# AMERICANA LIBRARY

ROBERT E. BURKE, EDITOR

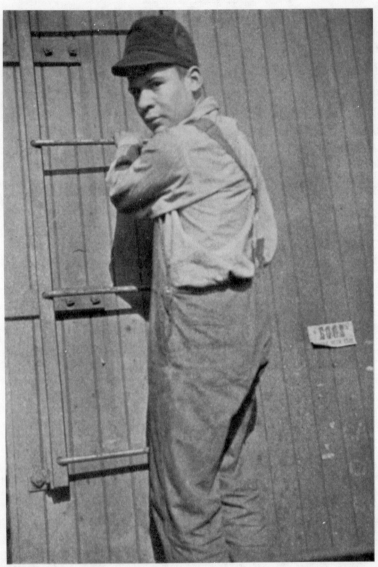

This boy had been on the road four years when we snapped this picture. He had started to board a standstill when he felt us looking at him from between the cars of a near-by movefast

# BOY AND GIRL TRAMPS OF AMERICA

By THOMAS MINEHAN

ILLUSTRATED WITH PHOTOGRAPHS BY THE AUTHOR

INTRODUCTION TO THE AMERICANA LIBRARY EDITION
BY DONALD W. WHISENHUNT

UNIVERSITY OF WASHINGTON PRESS
SEATTLE AND LONDON

Copyright © 1934 by Thomas Minehan
Originally published by Farrar and Rinehart, Inc. This edition
published by arrangement with Holt, Rinehart and Winston, Inc.
University of Washington Press Americana Library edition 1976
"Introduction to the 1976 Edition" by Donald W. Whisenhunt
copyright © 1976 by the University of Washington Press
Printed in the United States of America

Library of Congress Cataloging in Publication Data
Minehan, Thomas.
    Boy and girl tramps of America.

    (University of Washington Press Americana library edition;
29)
    Reprint with new introd. of the ed. published by Farrar and
Rinehart, New York.
    Includes bibliographical references.
    1. Children, Vagrant—United States. 2. United States—So-
cial conditions— 1933-1945. I. Title.
[HV4504.M5 1976]    362.7'3    76-7792
ISBN 0-295-95450-7

*TO MY MOTHER*

# CONTENTS

# LIST OF ILLUSTRATIONS

# INTRODUCTION TO THE 1976 EDITION

The existence of homeless people has been a feature of American life since the colonial period. These were usually people temporarily dislocated for one reason or another; many of them were on the move to the West where opportunity was supposedly greater. It was not until the advent of industrialization, however, that a new homeless class appeared. During the depression of the 1890s the hobo, or tramp, was first recognized as a serious social problem.[1]

Since that time a voluminous literature has developed concerning the tramp. One of the most difficult tasks was to properly define the homeless person. One approach has been to examine the motivation for choosing the wandering life. Some people rejected conventional, working society for a life of freedom on the road. Others, defeated by life, concluded that they could not fit into normal society. Periodically, especially with the intensification of industrialization, many more found themselves forced onto the road out of necessity. They moved from town to town as best they could seeking work. Regardless of their origin or reasons for leaving home, they became a part of that amorphous mass of humanity not normally seen or acknowledged by the larger society. They were drifters who were seen from time to time but very seldom considered ex-

1. See Robert H. Bremner, *From the Depths: The Discovery of Poverty in the United States* (New York: New York University Press, 1956), pp. 140-63.

cept by an occasional writer and by those whose profession it
was to care for the derelicts of society.

Various writers tried to distinguish between the wandering
groups by the names—hoboes, tramps, bums—that they gave
them. Others simply gave up and used the various names in-
terchangeably. According to some authorities, the so-called
professional wanderer was quite contemptuous of the temporary transients and thus resented being lumped together with
them.[2]

During the depression of the 1890s, the existence of tramps
was recognized by more people than ever before, partly because of the writings of Josiah Flynt and Owen Kildare. Both
men, authors of popular books about tramps, wrote from experience with great success. They studied tramps in great
detail and made the public aware of the problem.[3] As sociology
became more developed in the twentieth century, more thorough studies of this segment of the population were made.[4]
By the time of the Great Depression of the thirties, literature
was available for those who wished to know about the problem, but it is probably safe to assume that relatively few
Americans knew much, or cared to know much, about that
side of life.

The thirties, however, jolted the country out of its indifference. The economic collapse was so serious that the number of

2. Ibid.; Frederick Feied, *No Pie in the Sky: The Hobo as American Cul-
tural Hero in the Works of Jack London, John Dos Passos, and Jack Ke-
rouac* (New York: Citadel Press, 1964), pp. 7-19; Nels Anderson, *The
Hobo: The Sociology of the Homeless Man* (Chicago: University of Chicago Press, 1923).

3. Bremner, *From the Depths,* pp. 141-45.

4. See for example Anderson, *The Hobo;* Nels Anderson, *Men on the
Move* (Chicago: University of Chicago Press, 1940).

wandering people skyrocketed. In addition, the new homeless population took on new characteristics that bewildered social workers and public officials.

In the thirties, the transient population was composed of all types of people. Many were men who, finding opportunity nonexistent at home, were forced upon the road to seek work. Too often unsuccessful in their quest, they moved from town to town seeking that elusive goal—a job. Without resources, they were forced to travel as best they could—by foot, by hitch-hiking, or more commonly, by freight trains. Some, too embarrassed to return to anxious and hungry families, gave up the struggle altogether and became human flotsam on a sea of poverty. Others shouldered the burdens of responsibility and took their families with them. The common conception of these people resembled the Joads of John Steinbeck's *Grapes of Wrath*. However, there were many who were worse off and, indeed, might have felt themselves lucky to have the life of the Joads. These were the families on the road with few belongings and less hope and direction. They rode freight trains and begged their way from town to town. Under such conditions, the cohesion of the family unit was tenuous at best; the breakup of the family became a common occurrence.

The emergence of such a group was ignored as long as possible. Not only did they provide an embarrassment for the more prosperous, but they also represented a threat. The transients were a constant reminder that such a fate awaited virtually anyone who had a turn of bad luck. It would take very little to increase drastically the ranks of the less fortunate.

The existence of massive numbers of homeless people could not be totally ignored, but little serious effort was made to learn much about them. As a result, misunderstandings about

who these people were and what they represented abounded.
Harry Hopkins, prominent in the relief activities of the New
Deal, probably described them best.

They were industrial workers, artisans, laborers, who after years of
settled life, were forced by necessity to seek employment in new
places. They were dispossessed farmers, travelling westward with
their families as their fathers had done before them. They were
young men who never had a chance to work, and who could no
longer remain in dependence on their burdened parents. They
were country people looking for work in the city and city people
looking for security in the country. They were negroes, following
the usual road of opportunity northward. They were the aged, the
tuberculous and otherwise infirm, moving to the widely touted
climates of Florida, California and the Southwest in the hope that
a favorable climate would somehow mitigate the rigors of poverty.[5]

Associated with the difficulty of understanding the compo-
sition of this population was the related problem of learning
its size. Without an adequate count ever being made, esti-
mates ranged from those who said the number was small and
insignificant to those who believed that the transients num-
bered in the millions and constituted a real threat to American social order and stability. Without question, the number
was large; the threat they represented is another question altogether.

A large and significant segment of the homeless population
consisted of children. Of an estimated one and one-half to two
million transients in August 1932,[6] the Children's Bureau of

5. Harry L. Hopkins, *Spending to Save: The Complete Story of Relief*
(1936; reprint ed., Seattle: University of Washington Press, 1972), p. 126.
6. James Joseph Hannah, "Urban Reaction to the Great Depression in
the United States, 1929-1933" (Ph.D. dissertation, Department of History,
University of California, Berkeley, 1956), p. 120.

the Department of Labor calculated that 200,000 were children.[7] One month earlier an unnamed source had set the number at 300,000.[8] The exact number has never been ascertained, and probably never will be, but clearly it was significant. This group labeled as children included individuals ranging in age from their early twenties to as young as five or six.

Despite the general indifference, there were a number of contemporary studies, both professional and amateur, of the new transient population. Maury Maverick of San Antonio, at the time the tax collector of Bexar County and a rising political figure in Texas, made a personal tour throughout the state to investigate conditions among transients. After a relatively short excursion, he reported to Governor Ross Sterling the appalling conditions he found. He later wrote of his experiences in one chapter of his autobiography, *A Maverick American*.[9] In 1935 Nelson Algren, later to become famous as the author of such novels as *The Man With the Golden Arm*, wrote about transients in his first novel, *Somebody in Boots*.[10] Although the book is fiction, it is based upon Algren's own experiences as a youthful tramp. When he later recounted his experiences as a young man on the road, they resembled very closely the experiences of the characters in his novel.[11] Both Maverick and Algren spent more time with adult transients

7. Gilbert Seldes, *The Years of the Locust: America, 1929-1932* (1933; reprint ed., New York: Da Capo, 1973), p. 288.

8. *Austin Statesman,* 1 July 1932.

9. Maury Maverick, *A Maverick American* (New York: Covici, Friede, 1937).

10. Nelson Algren, *Somebody in Boots* (New York: Farrar, Straus & Giroux, 1935; Berkley Medallion paperback reprint, 1965).

11. H. E. F. Donohue, *Conversations with Nelson Algren* (New York: Hill and Wang, 1964).

xvi INTRODUCTION, 1976 EDITION

than with children, and their conclusions are of somewhat limited significance. Maverick's journeys were short and restricted to the state of Texas. Algren fictionalized his experiences based mostly on memory rather than a systematic study of these people. In addition, neither of them were trained observers of society.

The best contemporary study of the youthful transients was *Boy and Girl Tramps of America* by Thomas P. Minehan. Virtually forgotten now, it is one of the most moving accounts of the whole phenomenon of child tramps. It is proper and fitting that it be reprinted today.

Thomas Minehan had a varied career. Born in 1903 in Bird Island, Minnesota, he attended the University of Minnesota, where he took a B.A. in 1924 and an M.A. in 1933. During 1924-25 he taught in public schools in North Carolina. Following that stint, he was a free-lance journalist until 1930, when he became engaged in private business. In 1933 he became associated with the University of Minnesota, first as a research assistant in the Institute of Child Welfare and later as an instructor in sociology.[12] In 1935 he was named the director of reeducation for the State Department of Education.[13] Later, from 1945 to 1946, he was secretary to Congressman Frank Starkey of St. Paul. He died of a heart attack in 1948 at the Minneapolis home of his brother-in-law and sister, Mr. and Mrs. A. W. Shepard, where he had been living.[14]

Beginning during his business career and continuing for

12. Faculty Records Center, University of Minnesota to author, 9 November 1972.
13. *Minneapolis Tribune,* 19 May 1935.
14. *Minneapolis Times,* 10 May 1948.

sometime thereafter, Minehan became deeply interested in the plight of the homeless. At first, he studied them in a professional manner by interviews and by developing case studies, but he soon discovered that the transient wore a mask when talking to a sociological investigator. Like most people outside the mainstream of society, the transient gave the answers he believed the investigator wanted or else became belligerent and either exaggerated or discounted the seriousness of the situation. Therefore, to get a more accurate understanding of such a life, Minehan began to travel among the transients, concentrating especially on the younger ones, who accepted him as just another person on the move. In this procedure he followed the pattern established earlier by such people as Flynt and Kildare. The book reprinted here shows that his intermittent travels for two years were quite successful. In order to chronicle the activities as accurately as possible he used two techniques. First, since his trips were usually of short duration, he was able to make extensive notes just after an excursion when his memory was fresh. On other occasions when he was on the road for longer periods, he would occasionally slip away from the group and spend the night at a hotel where he could make notes in private of his impressions and conversations.

As he says in the Introduction, his original plan was to write a sociological study of the transient based on his travels. He soon discovered, however, that he could not report his findings in cold statistics and case studies. The lives of the children were much too personal to be plotted on graphs and charts. Therefore, he decided to write the book in a narrative form, even on occasion resembling a diary. The result is the book reprinted here.

*Boy and Girl Tramps of America* received generally good reviews. Most critics praised Minehan for forcing the reading public to recognize a situation that it would rather ignore. Some reviewers thought it significant that an academic man took to the road himself for a firsthand view of the situation rather than rely upon cold, unemotional, official statistics and secondhand reports.[15] One critic, not so impressed, felt that Minehan distorted and exaggerated the condition of the youthful tramps because he seemed to be writing with Hollywood in mind.[16] Others criticized his writing ability,[17] but the *New York Times* commended his approach. "Congratulations are due . . . that he did not attempt to make literature out of the material he has put into this book. . . . For life is of more consequence than literature, and the gruesome pieces of certain of its aspects that he has collected and exhibits here in all their significance deserve the most anxious attention."[18]

Of all the reviews, probably the one in the *Christian Century* grasped the long-range significance best.

In the post-war days of prosperity and gin, youth expressed its frustrations in drink and sexual promiscuity. Today, it wanders on the road. Thus we may come to realize a social problem that will be with us the duration of these young people's lives, but with the consciousness that even if these boys and girls survive the despair, brutality and terror of life on the road, they will survive only with scars that do not easily heal.[19]

With a book of such significance, the question of its almost

15. *Books,* 8 July 1934, p. 1.
16. *Survey,* January 1935, p. 26.
17. *New Republic,* 1 August 1934, p. 323.
18. *New York Times,* 1 July 1934, p. 10.
19. *Christian Century,* 5 September 1934, p. 1117.

total obscurity today is a legitimate one. There seems to be no satisfactory answer. As the prosperity of war replaced depression, Americans were most concerned about defeating the enemy and regaining some of the physical comforts lost during the previous decade. The depression was a painful experience best forgotten by those who had so recently passed through it. In the postwar world other national and international problems captured the attention of the country. Americans were more concerned about national survival, the ensuring of a continued prosperity, and a myriad of other interests, rather than remembering those grim days of the recent past.

Historians, too, have generally ignored the problem of transiency in the depression. Most historians seemed more comfortable writing about New Deal programs and other more exciting events of the thirties. Undoubtedly, one of the factors in the reluctance to study the tramps was the elusiveness of the primary sources. Unfortunately, such valuable studies as Minehan's were forgotten. As yet, no systematic study of the problem of transiency during the thirties has been made.

With this in mind, the reissuing of *Boy and Girl Tramps of America* is all the more important. Despite its weaknesses, it is the best firsthand account available. Minehan not only recounts the conditions under which the young tramps lived, but he includes chapters on why they left home, how they traveled, how they acquired food and clothing, and on their attitudes toward sex and religion. He even includes a chapter tracing the history of vagabondage. The spice of the book, of course, is his inclusion of conversations with and among the young tramps. By reading them, one gets a flavor of the times, generally, and of the life of the tramp, specifically.

Minehan's accuracy seems trustworthy. He wrote from his fisthand notes with the desire to give a true picture of transient life. He appears to have had no reason to distort or exaggerate the conditions he found. Even if one were to assume that a motive of the book was to promote a specific public policy with regard to the transients, his conclusions still seem valid when compared with other sources. For example, the books of Maverick and Algren, even though they deal with a different group of transients, basically substantiate Minehan's conclusions. In fact, the three books overlap enough in content that they corroborate one another.

The reappearance of this book comes at a propitious time for another reason. During the past decade a new wave of transiency appeared on the American scene. On first glance, it would be simple to call this recent increase a modern manifestation of the thirties, but even a superficial study discredits this interpretation.

It is not possible to examine the sixties and seventies on the same terms as the thirties. True, they were both periods of social upheaval, but the causes of transiency were different. The sixties and seventies have not been a period of depression; there have been jobs available even if they have not been exactly what the contemporary transient seeks. Today's traveler may have left home because of parental conflicts as did many of those in the thirties, but in most cases the cause was probably not economic. The great majority today can go home without putting a financial burden on their parents. Many seem to be on the road today as something of a lark. They play the game by their dress and fashions. They wander the country for limited periods without any plan to make it a permanent life. If they are bums or tramps, it is usually by choice. The youthful tramp of the thirties was not there by choice.

Each group reflects something about the nature of the United States. When there is economic or social upheaval the number of transients seems to increase. Perhaps this is a modern manifestation of the frontier spirit in an age when the frontier has long since disappeared. During the thirties, the editor of a Texas newspaper described the transients as "simply pioneers in a land that needs pioneers no longer."[20] This was a charitable view, but this editor may have been more correct than he knew. Sociologists have told us that rootlessness is an American characteristic and historians have chronicled it for us. We are a people with a vague longing to be on the move. It may take only a slight challenge to our security to cause us to take to the road, whether it be by automobile, camper, hitchhiking, or by catching the nearest freight train. Therefore, even though direct comparison between the thirties and the past decade is inconclusive, the wandering young people of each period do reflect something of the strain upon the social fabric. Interpretation of these social phenomena still remains the major task of the historian.

Minehan performed a highly commendable job in reporting the life of the child tramp in the thirties. His account makes it easier to understand how such a phenomenon could occur, but, more importantly, it forces us today to realize and admit that it did actually occur. Minehan was a first-rate reporter on the tramps of the thirties; one can only hope that someone else is doing the same for today's transients.

DONALD W. WHISENHUNT

Portales, New Mexico
May 1976

20. *Austin Statesman,* 17 October 1931.

## INTRODUCTION TO THE ORIGINAL EDITION

In company with millions of other Americans who have heard the panhandlers' plea for a couple of nickels for a cup of coffee, I often wondered what the man who is down and out thinks of us and of our civilization. Unlike the ordinary citizen, I had the professional time as well as the personal inclination to investigate. Three years ago I began to collect case histories of men who went down with the boom in 1929. But case histories gave me little inkling into the inner mind of the man on the bread line. When I asked the men what they thought they tried to anticipate my own ideas, thereby enhancing their chances of obtaining a dime. Truth in regard to the homeless man, I decided, could never be ascertained in this manner.

And how could it be ascertained? Were the men, I asked myself, any more truthful with each other? Would a man living on the relief line learn more than an investigator talking to men on the streets or to social cases across an interviewer's desk? One evening in November, 1932, I disguised myself in old clothes and stood in a bread line in the cold and rain.

The experience was memorable. I can still see the ragged cold line of men shivering in the rain and slime

of an alley.   They seemed like some strange night
creatures who stirred abroad from caves and water holes.
In the rain and fog I heard them talk, and their talk was
not as other men's, nor as I had heard it on the main
stem.   Gone was the whine of the panhandler and the
boastful attitude of the bum.   In their own element, the
flotsam and jetsam of our economic system seemed no
different from other men.

And yet there was a difference.   There was present,
not only in their conversations but in their very postures
a subcurrent of fear and anxiety, a sullen acceptance of
life, a bitter apathy, absent from the attitudes and conversations of other men.

We inched down the alley in the gloom and into a
dimly lighted hole where we were given a moldy cheese
sandwich and a cup of what the men appropriately
enough called "misery."   Silent, huddled, we munched
our food and gulped the coffee.   Over us stood an argus-
eyed attendant who had lost not a single cup in thirty
years of mission work.   Out into rain and wind we stumbled to stand again in dejected groups in darkened door-
ways and under the eaves of buildings.   And the talk
of the men was not the talk it had been on the main
stem.

Here I decided was a possibility of getting ideas, attitudes, and viewpoints of the mass of men hit most cruelly
by the depression.   In my spare time I began to associate with them, dressed always like another homeless
wanderer.   And I learned things which could not be

learned in any other way and ascertained opinions and attitudes not to be ascertained by other methods.[1]

One of the first facts I learned was that a great number of homeless men were youths and even boys. By day hordes of unemployed men loitered about the missions and bread lines—marginal laborers looking for work in the slave markets, unemployed local men, chronic bums, and transients. Many were old. Some were crippled. All were down and out. At night bands of youths, too proud to be seen lingering in the sunlight with "old bums," came in for a bowl of beans and a flop.

And as I left the mission district to live in hobo railroad yard camps or jungles and river shanty-towns, I found more and more youths and not a few girls. In the railroad yards I waited near a block signal where freights from Chicago and the South stopped. Mobs of men got off every train. Many were not youths, but boys. And some were girls—children really—dressed in overalls or army breeches and boys' coats or sweaters —looking, except for their dirt and rags, like a Girl Scout club on an outing.

Where were their homes? Where were they going? How long had they been on the road? Why did they leave home? What did they expect to do in the future? I began asking questions.

How did they live? What did they eat? Where

---

[1] See, "A Study of Attitudes of Transient Men and Boys," by Thomas Minehan—a Thesis, University of Minnesota, 1933.

did they sleep? How did they get clothing? What did they do all day? I began living with them.

Before I stopped living with them and asking questions, I had collected case histories of over five hundred boys and girls, associated on terms of intimacy and equality with several thousand, traveled in six states as a transient, experienced in all seasons and under all conditions the daily life of a boy or girl living in box cars. Two years had elapsed.

I did not, of course, live with them continuously or consecutively. I am neither a boy nor a tramp. I am a sociologist, interested in man and in how he reacts to his environment. I might have gone to Africa to study the influence of environment upon man or to Russia to record the reaction of youth to social change. Yet it was not necessary. Here in America man was reacting to his environment and youth was experiencing as great a change in homes as in Russia. The changes in America were not directed, nor were they caused by external forces such as invasion. They were the result of economic and social pressure within the group itself. For that very reason they might be more significant, more interesting. Here was the possibility of a new, strange field of investigation. To it I turned my energies. My plan was to associate with as many homeless persons as possible under conditions of social equality, to experience their life, to record their stories, to ascertain in as scientific a manner as possible their opinions, ideas, and attitudes.

To accomplish this it was necessary to take notes. I could not take notes while living with the group. After associating with them at missions for a day, or traveling in box cars for a week-end, I went to a room and jotted down my impressions, returned to my classes at the University of Minnesota, and at the first opportunity discarded my school clothes for the rags of a vagrant. Week-ends, holidays, and vacations found me away from home. During the summers of 1932 and 1933 I spent considerable time on the road, chiefly in the Middle West.

In the fall of 1933, I had a thick dossier full of notes and impressions, 500 life histories of boys and girls I had met on the bum, 1,000 samples of conversations, and over 2,500 opinions, ideas, and attitudes expressed by all classes of transients under all conditions. What did my investigation reveal?

In conventional sociological form I drew up my tables, analyzed the data statistically, worked a few correlations . . . I was following approved technique. Yet, the analysis was unsatisfactory. It seemed totally inadequate to say that 324 youths left home because the father was unemployed and unable to support his family. Less adequate it seemed to say that fourteen boys in need of shoes had to steal to get them or that nine hungry girls had to sell their bodies for bread. Scenes of boys on the road, pictures of girls in box cars kept pushing into my mind to cry against the facts I had tabulated so carefully and arranged on such neat graphs.

I remembered the girl who shared my sheepskin on a cold and blustering night, the boy who stole a shirt for me, and the older transient who almost broke his neck trying to get a package of Bull Durham so that I might have a decent smoke. . . .

These were not so many cases to be analyzed, so many sticks to be counted and arranged in sequential order. They were boys and girls, flesh-and-blood youngsters who should be in high schools and homes and were in box cars and jungles. I had seen pictures of the Wild Children of revolution-racked Russia. I had read of the free youth of Germany after the World War. I knew that in every nation, following a plague, an invasion, or a revolution, children left without parents and homes became vagrants.

Before my own experiences I had always believed that in America we managed things better. And yet in the face of economic disorganization and social change our own youth took to the highroad.

To describe their life in statistical terms was not only inadequate, it was untrue. Such a description omitted the most important phases of their lives, their strife against cold, their battle for bread, their struggle to obtain and repair clothing, their hates, their humors, and their loves. . . .

An artist—not a scientist—was needed to paint what I had seen, record what I had heard. And I was not even an amateur craftsman. Yet for the sake of the homeless thousands of boys and girls, I decided to try.

In my descriptions in the following pages I have relied upon actual incidents and real characters for material. Nothing has been substantially changed; nothing added. My attempt has been to portray the life of migrant youth in America as I saw and experienced it.

BOY AND GIRL
TRAMPS OF
AMERICA

# I

THE freight jerks wheezily to a stop in the early autumn twilight. Southbound, the majority of transients remain in chair cars. Fifty or sixty, transferring for Chicago and points east, drop off, skirt the station, and head for the main stem of a small division point town.

Two automobiles shoot out into the middle of the street effectively blocking the first intersection. Five men alight. Four carry ominous-looking pick handles. The fifth smokes an authoritative cigar and swaggers confidently. As at a command, the van of transients halts. The rear crowds up. Huddled stupidly together like sheep, we stand silently as a stock truck carrying more men with more pick handles swings into the street behind.

The stout man without a club and with the cigar steps forward, flashes a sheriff's badge, and speaks. "You are under arrest, boys, come along."

He speaks quietly, but there is in his voice a vibrant quality as though he were daring us to disobey. We press closer together, stupid, silent. A few furtively glance about for paths of escape, but see none. New to the road, a pockmarked boy of thirteen whimpers a little like a forlorn puppy.

3

"Under arrest, boys," the sheriff repeats slowly, coming step by step nearer, "but don't let that scare you. We aren't going to be tough on you unless you make us tough. We aren't going to put you in any rotten old jail all winter or in a chain gang on the roads if you treat us fair. But you can't panhandle this town, boys. You can't panhandle this town. Remember that!

"The last freight has just pulled out of here. There ain't another one along until eight o'clock tomorrow morning. I got a offer to make you. How would you like to get a nice supper, a good warm bed, a nice breakfast and be out of here in time to catch that morning train?

"Well, that's my offer to you.

"You're under arrest, boys, but we won't hold you after tomorrow morning if you come quietly. We'll take you to jail, feed you a good warm supper, give you a nice bed, a nice shower bath if you want it, a good place to shave before breakfast, and then you get out in time to catch that Chicago train.

"What do you say?"

What did we say?

What could we say?

Five men drop from the truck at our rear. Four deputies preceded by the sheriff lead the way to the town jail.

It is half a mile through the graying twilight. From shop windows and front porches townspeople stare at us. They are neither hostile, curious, nor concerned. They just stare as they would stare at a man driving hogs through town.  Our plight does not concern them.

A brown-haired girl of seven in neat dimity and long curls is teaching a two-year-old brother to speak.  She points at us through a picket fence while her little fat-faced brother stares.

"Bum!" she says unemotionally.  "Bum!  Bum!  Say 'bum,' Donald.  Bum!  Dirty!  Ugly, ugh!"

Donald just stares.

Halfway to the calaboose, a young, nervous chap, sophisticated perhaps in the food of jails, makes a dive for liberty.  He is quick, but a guard is quicker.  A pick handle fetches him a rap on the shin.  He falls to the pavement ki-yi-ing like a stoned dog.  The other guards close about us in happy anticipation of a fight in which they can't lose.  The sheriff alone is unperturbed and judicial.

"Now there's no use in trying that, boys," he says.  "Just come along quietly and you'll get a better meal than you could panhandle."

We come.

The jail is an old stone and stucco structure painted a leprous yellow with a newer sheriff's quarters of flamingo brick.  We pass through a narrow hallway in the sheriff's addition, past a kitchen from which rise odors of cooking food, and enter a square exercise bull pen.  Gates clang shut behind us.  We are in jail.

The sheriff's wife comes to the grating after a few minutes.  She peers at us as though we were monkeys in a zoo. "How many of you are there?" she asks. "We'll have supper ready in half an hour."

There are, as ten separate counts agree, fifty-four. And forty are under twenty-one; seven are less than sixteen, four are over fifty, three are World War veterans. In better times and better clothing, the youths might be high school or college students attending an out-of-town game.

No furniture adorns the small room. Not a bench circles the wall. The boy tramps, tired and hungry, collapse on the floor. Some stretch out on stomachs, faces pillowed on arms. Others stand dejectedly leaning against the walls. The majority have been through the works many times. They know jail food and jail beds.

Fifteen minutes pass. Twenty. The sheriff returns with two deputies.

"Now, boys," he says, and the Lord Chancellor of England in his black robes and white wig was never more solemn, "if you'll all pass out this door one at a time and into this here cell block we'll serve supper to you in a few minutes. We're going to search you boys; so if you got any knives or guns on you, you better give them up. You can have them back in the morning. We just don't want anybody starting a fight or getting cut up in the cell block tonight. And if you got any money, better check that too. Check everything, especially razors, that you don't need until morning. In the morning we'll give you your razors and your packs, and your knives as you check out."

The sheriff's wife and another dumpy girl sit at a table near the door. They have several checking stubs well used, which they give to each man having any "valuables." These are thrown indiscriminately into a rusty washtub. The search is thorough and complete. An hour passes before the men cross from the bullpen into the cell block.

The cells are all locked. Four are occupied by drunks in various stages of post-intoxication; one by a ratty little bigamist in enormous horn-rimmed glasses, looking, as Texas remarks, "like a Ford in super-balloon tires." A small one-seat toilet jutting out at the end of the hall is the only article of decoration or convenience. The men stand in line. It is dark. Four dim bulbs illuminate the corridors. We slump in tired but non-protesting dejection on the sheet steel floor. The echo of a locomotive whistle comes through the early fall air. It stirs vague longings in the hearts of the young child tramps. A flare of interest passes over the life-lashed faces of many.

"And I could of been on her front blind," regrets Bill.

"You'd freeze there," says Candles, the boy who had tried to escape, as he inspects his black and blue shins.

"If he would," says Texas, "he'd freeze in Africa. If you know how to ride them blinds are warm."

They argue, listlessly and without spirit.

Silence again.

The cell inmates prepare for bed. A drunk removes all his clothes save shoes and hat. He tries to spread the blanket over his feet, but as he turns sideways, he encounters difficulties. We laugh at him but without mirth.

"Why don't you get sent to jail," a man in another cell asks us, "and get treated like a white guy? Three square meals a day and nothing to do but play poker with the sheriff and kid his wife. Wait until you see what they feed *you*."

We haven't long to wait. The sheriff's wife, her assistant, and the two deputies enter, pulling our supper on two small red coaster wagons. We line up, a long serpent of men and boys stretching hungrily around the cell corridor and back until the first man is within hand-shaking distance of the last. Each transient, as he passes the coaster wagon, is given a pie tin upon which is heaped the warm supper promised by the sheriff. It consists of one cup of cold tomatoes, mostly juice, one cold boiled potato with the scabrous jacket still on, one slice of muggy bread. I smile at the sheriff's wife. She gives me two small potatoes and an extra half-slice of bread.

"How are chances to get something to drink?" asks a man whose pie tin leaks. Unable to sop his bread in the tomato juice, he has difficulty swallowing.

"Shut up, you goddam ungrateful bum, you," curses the deputy. "Don't you appreciate what you're getting for nothing? If you don't like it—"

"Frank—" The sheriff's wife is speaking.

"That's all right, boys," she assures us, "I'll see that you have something to drink before I leave."

She does. We have three tin cups and a wash boiler full of water. A deputy turns out all but two corridor lights, collects the pie tins, and bids us a not unpleasant good night.

"And now," remarks Texas, hardened young road kid of fifteen, "after our nice warm supper we'll crawl into a nice warm bed."

"Why," asks Bill, "do they always have to have sour bread in jails?"

"Why do they have to have jails?"

"Or sheriffs."

"Or hard times."

"Or bums."

"God! I don't believe that anybody knows what it is all about."

"We come and we go," says an old man. "Where the hell we come from or why and where the hell we are going nobody cares and nobody knows."

The discussion becomes philosophically pessimistic. We sit upon the floor and tell sad stories of the death of dreams.

"You're creaking the springs," growls one of the boys, trying to sleep at the end of the corridor. Our eyes, like the eyes of tired dogs dozing, fasten upon the dim bulbs. Soon all is silent.

Stretched out in his rags on the steel floor every man

and boy is trying to sleep. A few remove shoes, which they tie to their wrists so that nobody can "trade."

An old aristocratic-appearing man picks at a callus on the ball of his foot with half a razor blade. The blade slips. His foot bleeds. Unable to check the blood, he hops to the end of the corridor and sticks his foot into the toilet flush bowl. Five minutes later he passes by me again, and I see his bleary, insane eyes. He is muttering to himself: "But, Mary, if you would only let me explain, Mary. If you'd only let me explain. Mary, why, if I could explain . . ."

I remove a sweater from under my second shirt and spread it on the floor. Texas and I lay our faces on it. The trick of sleeping on a steel floor is to sleep the first half of the night on your stomachs with your hands and arms free. Later, you may roll over on one side, crook an arm for a pillow or sleep on the back with your hands under your head; but if you sleep on hands or arms all night you will have stiff and painful joints next day.

Our pallet is directly in front of a small cell housing a drunk. He is coming out of the liquor. Texas has removed his cap. Curly chestnut hair gleams in the dim light. His face, flushed in the first relaxation of sleep, is as soft as a baby's.

The drunk, his face scarred from many and mighty liquor battles, waddles to the door.

"Say," he says to Texas, in a voice rasping through

an alcohol-burned larynx, "did you ever have a mother?"

Texas, half asleep, does not answer.

"Did you ever have a mother?"

I stir irritatedly. The drunk perceives that I am awake.

"You had a mother, didn't you?" he asks. "Of course you had. I can tell by looking at you that you had a mother."

I turn my face away, hoping that he will shut up.

"And a fine old lady, I'll bet she was, too." He goes on sentimentally in that voice which is all throaty inarticulation. "We all had mothers. Where would we be if it wasn't for mothers? All that I have, all that I ever am going to have I owe to Mother. And you, too, Shorty. Don't you ever forget that. All that you have you owe to her."

"For cripes sake, let me sleep," I mutter.

"And you know what your mother is doing tonight?" the drunk continues. "She is sitting by a window waiting for her wandering boy. Where is my wandering boy tonight? And you know where he is? Sleepin' on the floor of a jail house. Sleepin' on the floor of a jail house."

"Pipe down, sailor," orders the man next to me, an ex-ironmolder from Youngstown.

"Shut your goddam mouth," says Texas, as he opens one eye.

"All right," agrees the drunk, strangely amiable,

"I'll pipe down, I'll shut up, but you're sleepin' on the floor of a jail house just the same, and don't you forget it."

We don't. Nobody who has once slept on an all-steel bed ever forgets it. But we sleep anyway. Outside thunder and lightning and rain and a cold autumn wind. Inside fourteen men and forty boys, free and honorable American citizens, sleep on the steel floors of jail corridors while five law violators enjoy mattresses and blankets in cells.

Morning comes. A deputy wakes us at five o'clock. He brings in three tin washbasins, an armful of newspapers for towels, and a bar of laundry soap for shaving. It is hard, caustic soap and in cold water lathers weakly into suds which evaporate upon touching the beard. Still we shave, hacking and chopping patiently and without pain or complaint at the stubble. The razors are dull. Our faces, toughened by wind and rain, have lost their civilized sensitivity. We care little whether beard is chopped off or pulled out.

And now breakfast.

First the men in the cells are fed. They receive a bowl of oatmeal with milk and sugar, two fried eggs and strips of bacon, two slices of buttered toast, a dish of prunes, and a cookie. With, of course, coffee. We receive a cupful of watery cornmeal mush on the unwashed pie tin of last night and a slice of dry bread. And again the bread is sour.

Train time approaches. The men become restive. But

there is no cause for fear. The sheriff and his deputies arrive in time, march us through town and into a box car of a freight waiting in the siding. As solicitous as a man bidding an unwelcome relative good-bye, he remains until the mail thunders by and the freight with many protesting groans pulls out.

The sun comes up, a warm caressing sun of early autumn. Some child tramps, still weary, sleep in the ends of the box car. Four play rummy with a soiled deck of cards, while another four kibitz. Texas, Happy Joe and I sit at the door of the box car, watching the passing panorama of the rural countryside. Here is a man fall-plowing, another discing a field. Truck gardeners at another farm are loading potatoes. In an orchard a whole family packs apples. The freight gathers speed. We will be in Chicago by nightfall.

"And why," Texas asks, echoing my thoughts, "Chicago?"

"That's what I say," agrees Jack, an extremely muscular young boy from the coal fields of Pennsylvania.

"Let's take our time about hitting the main drag," suggests Bill from Buffalo. "All we'll get in town is sermons and sour stew."

"And a nice soft bed on the mission floor," adds Happy Joe, an Italian from New York. "I know a better place."

Two hours later ten of us drop off the train at a water tower. We hike up the road a quarter of a mile before cutting through woods to an old deserted limestone quarry. Water has filled one of the pits, forming a natural pool. Delightful clear, limpid water, it is indescribably exhilarating as we remove our clothes and plunge in for a swim. A little cold with the first tang of fall, the water, as Happy says, "scrubs out the jail smell."

Later the limestone rocks, pleasantly warm with the sun of Indian summer, are softer than the bed we slept in last night. We wash socks, shirts, and underwear. On the warm rocks they dry in an hour. And on the warm rocks we relax and sneak a little nap while our clothes air.

Refreshed and dressed an hour later, we are ravenously hungry. There is a jungle, or hobo camp, on the banks of the Illinois about half a mile away where we can find tins for cooking and shelter from prying eyes.

To it we turn our steps.

On the way we encounter another band of youthful vagrants. Five boys and two girls have dropped off a Big Four freight. They are headed for the same rendezvous.

One girl is a tall, spindly lass, indistinguishable at a distance from a boy. Her black hair is cut like a man's and parted on the left, and her face is as tanned as an Indian's. Overalls and an O. D. shirt open at the neck reveal no curves. Heavy army shoes are worn down to the counters on both heels. The other girl is a curly-haired blonde, with an evident fondness for boys. She wears riding breeches, cloth puttees, tennis shoes, and a dirty sweat shirt.

When we arrive at the jungles, the lanky girl takes command. "This," she sniffs, inspecting the dirty lubricating cans left by the previous gang, "is a hell of a way to leave things."

"Here, you, Blimp," she orders, "take these tins down to the river and scour them out with sand. You, Jimmy, get some wood, and Tubby for God's sake take a bath. The rest of you gaffers," she looks sternly at us, "get some grub. I'll cook it."

An unwritten rule of hobo land forbids panhandling or stealing within a mile of a jungle. A mile or more away, Texas and I came upon a man digging potatoes.

"Will you give us a few, please, mister," I ask, "if we dig three or four bushel for you?"

The man and his wife stare at us.

"We ain't had nothing to eat since last night," adds Texas, smiling a frightened half-smile.

"Sure," says the farmer.

We fill two bushel baskets of potatoes.

"Live near?" inquires the man.

"No," says Texas, "we're from Chicago. Went West to thresh. Made no money. Now we're hiking home."

There is talk of crops and Kansas. The farmer whispers something to his wife. She goes to the house. We fill three or four more baskets with potatoes, helping the man load a truck. The wife returns with a pot of steaming coffee and a picnic basket lunch. And what a lunch!

Ham and egg sandwiches, buttered bread, two kinds of jelly, a dozen apples, fresh homemade cookies, and half a cake.

Lunch over, we finish loading the truck. The farmer offers us all the potatoes we can carry. His wife insists that we have a loaf of fresh bread and a glass of her jelly. We ask for a head of cabbage, receive three, and obtain permission to pick all the apples we can carry. Our burlap sack bulges as we carry it on a stick between us and "high-tail" down the sun-streaked road to camp.

The other boys have been just as successful. There is food for a platoon. One brings four fish which he received from a sportsman, another, arriving after dark, three chickens, and a fourth a large chunk of salt pork, a gift for helping a farmer milk. Three boys help the girls prepare the food.

The camp-fires leap gaily as our hearts. The stars twinkle kindly in a cobalt sky. The air has in it a threat of frost, but we care not. Full of food and near a warm fire we are happy and content. There are lean-to's of willows and scrap tin to which we can retreat if it rains. No need to worry about cops and sheriffs, nor snoopy case workers at Welfare stations and hell-shouting ministers at missions. When it becomes colder we will have to follow once more the depressing routine of organized charity and be kicked from town to town, as we stand hungry and cold in bread lines, but no need to worry now. When it gets colder—

"When it gets colder," says Texas very sensibly, "we'll go to California."

But we do not go to California, nor do we live always like carefree young scavengers on the fringe of society, and it becomes colder—much, much colder.

Texas and I separate. He flips a manifest one night as the cops drive me from the yards, and we meet in northern Iowa on a freezing December day just before Christmas. A municipal rat hole is the place of meeting.

Blue with cold and very lonely he still wears his tattered gray coat and patched blue pants with an air. He steps proudly down the stairs and his supple body is still graceful. His keen blue eyes seek a familiar face in the room. He is glad to see me.

Texas has just come from North Dakota. He has no shoes. Paper swathed in cocoon folds inside a pair of man's old rubber boots keeps his feet from freezing. He has not been so fortunate with his ears. Both were frozen in Minot. They bulge out from the side of his head, a black and massive eruption, cut with livid blood scars and streaks of yellow matter.

Tough as he is, Texas winces as he removes the odd contraption made out of a wheat sack and a piece of rabbit fur that serves as cap. He smiles at me. Two front teeth are missing.

"I lost them," he explains as he cups his hands and blows on them, "in an argument with a shack on the Sante Fé. He tried to kick me off but I did the kicking. And so I won the argument but I lost my teeth."

The room is a jabbering rookery of men and boys who keep stumbling in out of the bitter cold that cuts like frozen razor blades through thinly clad bodies to the marrow of the bone. The men caw and dance grotesquely as with stamping of feet and untidy flapping of sleeves they pound circulation and blood back into semi-frozen limbs while every transient tries to tell every other one how cold it was on the train he just rode. An enormous gong sounds. Subdued and silent as convicts, we march into the dining room where we receive a slice of stale bread, a spoonful of beans in a bowl of water and an order to leave town before breakfast.

We may, the manager informs us magnanimously, sleep on the cement floor until five o'clock.

"And if we don't get out of town—" A boy new to the road is desperate and defiant.

"You'll get this," answers a city detective, slapping the boy. Caught off balance, the youth folds up like a camp chair, striking his face against a bench on the way to the floor. He quivers spasmodically in his rags, face down on the dirty cement floor now being stained scarlet.

The heavy-foot, who has had supper with us and been spying upon us all afternoon, inquires pleasantly, "Anybody else want anything?"

Nobody does. The boy rises to one knee. His hand seizes a bench. Blood pours from his nose and bubbles from his mouth as his eyes seek wildly in the room for one friend. We stare back in stupid incomprehension.

The heavy-foot steps forward. With one hand he

grips the boy's thin shoulder, lifts him up and spins him into a seat roughly but not unkindly.

"I didn't try to sock you, Jack," he half-apologizes, "if I did you'd still be out.  But we can't take any lip"— he looks at all of us with eyes as merciless as a machine gun—"and you gotta get out of town before breakfast."

We get.

It is spring when I see Texas again.  Farmers are planting sugar beets in Wisconsin as our freight pulls west.

Gaunt as a wild animal wintering in the uplands where forage is poor, Texas has lost another tooth.  The upper third of one ear has permanently disappeared.  The other is flattened in the cauliflower of a prize fighter's. He walks with an odd irregular stiffness from too much sleeping in box cars on zero nights and too much walking and too little food.  Water runs from both eyes.  The lower lids sag strangely for a boy, and his face has in it the harsh lines of age.  He shakes hands with me.  Two fingers feel stiff.

"I busted the mitt," Texas says, "in a fight with a Nashville shack.  He wore brass knucks.  I threw my hand up to guard my face"—he illustrates—"and he cracks two fingers.

"I've been ducking cops and chain gangs all winter in the South."  His eyes automatically scan the men in the car for heavy-foots.  "After freezing my ears, I decided to get out of the North if I had to go to jail.

But I got by. The stem is pretty tough all through the South. I kept moving. I got by."

"And now what?" I ask him as the train jerks and then rattles forward.

"Oh, anything." There is defiance but not despair in his voice. "I can't get a job anywhere. I can't get in the CCC because I have no dependents. I can't remain in any state unless I go to a slave camp, and that is that. What chance have I got? Less chance than a man with two wooden legs in a forest fire. I've seen a lot of the country in the last year, and I'm glad I've seen it but if a guy travels too much he becomes a bum, *and I don't want to be a bum.*"

# II

## BEFORE THE BIG TROUBLE CAME

"IT wasn't so bad at home," says Texas to me in the early weeks of our wandering, "before the big trouble came." The other boys have gone to sleep. Texas and I are sitting on a log near a jungle campfire and talk of other days.

"Before the big trouble came," he goes on and his eyes are somber in the firelight. "We got along pretty good. Dad, of course, never was very well. He was in the war and he got some kind of sickness, I guess, but he couldn't get a pension. He was always sick for about a month every year, and that meant that he had to look for a new job each time he got well. If he had been husky it might have been easy to get a good job, but he was kinda small and then sick you know.

"But we got along swell before the big trouble came even if there were seven of us kids. I shined shoes in a barber shop. Jim carried papers. And Marie took care of Mrs. Rolph's kids. Mother always did some sewing for the neighbors. We had a Chevvie and a radio and a piano. I even started to high school mornings, the year the big trouble came.

"Dad got sick as usual but we never thought anything of it. When he comes to go back to work he can't get a job, and everybody all of a sudden-like seems to be hard up. I cut the price of shines to a nickel but it didn't help much. I even used to go around and collect shoes and shine them at the houses or take them away, shine and return them, but even then some weeks I couldn't make a dime.

"Mrs. Rolph's husband got a cut and she cans Marie. Jim had to quit the paper route because he lost all his cash customers, and the others never paid. Nobody wanted Mother to sew anything. And there we were, seven of us kids and Dad and Mother, and we couldn't make a cent like we could before the big trouble came."

Texas pushes a piece of birch into the fire. I throw in a pine knot. The embers crackle and hiss. A cone of sparks and white smoke rises straight into the air. The smoke turns darker. There is a pungent smell of resin as the pine knot flames and burns. The night is becoming cold. We nudge closer to the fire, warming our shins. Texas stretches his hands, slender and delicate as a girl's, strong as a pianist's, toward the flame. As in a spectroscope I can see the metatarsal bones and the blue outline of veins and the heavier muscle fibers throbbing in the firelight.

Were his hands, I ask myself, so slender and translucent before the big trouble came—before that monstrous depression, that economic juggernaut that was to crash through his home, cast him out upon the road, and make him perhaps a bum for life?

"But the big trouble came," he continues, caressing

his chin with warm palms, "and there we were. Oh, we tried hard enough, and everybody did their best. Marie made the swellest wax flowers. The kids peddled ironing cloths. Mother tried to sell some homemade bakery, and Dad did everything. We did our best, I guess, but it wasn't good enough, for the big trouble had come and nobody had any money.

"Dad gave up pipe smoking in the fall. All last winter we never had a fire except about once a day when Mother used to cook some mush or something. When the kids were cold they went to bed. I quit high school of course, but the kids kept going because it didn't cost anything and it was warm there.

"In February I went to Fort Worth. Mother used to know a man there, and she thought maybe he could help me get a job. But he was as hard up as anybody else. I didn't want to return home and pick bread off the kids' plate so I tried to get work for a farmer for my board. Instead, I got a ride to California. Near Salinas I worked in the lettuce fields, cutting and washing lettuce. I made $32 and I sent $10 home. But that was my first and last pay check. I got chased out of California in June."

The fire flickers and ebbs. We pull a night log into the embers and prepare to join our companions in sleep. I turn my back to the fire and face the eternal stars.

"Since then," concludes Texas and his voice sounds far away and distant as Arcturus blinking unconcernedly down on me, "I just been traveling."

"My old man was crippled in the Lackawanna shops," Jennie, a dumpy Hungarian girl from Pennsylvania, is talking one morning as we tidy up the jungle before flipping a freight. "Dumb and scared to death, he didn't get a cent except a promise of a lifetime job. They kept him four years, until the hard times came. After that he never got a job except for a few months as city watchman. Mother worked nights, cleaning an office building. We kids used to go and help her and keep her company. But she couldn't stand it all the time. They took her to the hospital one morning, and three days later she died. Father said they gave her the Black Bottle because she was poor, but I don't think so, do you? I think she was just all in.

"Dad tried to keep a home for the four of us kids. Cripes! he was as good as any man could be, considering. But what could he do? I was willing to work but nobody hired me and the rest of the kids were too young. So a home took the three kids, my married sister in Allentown took my father, and I just sort of scrammed.

"I never had much chance to go to school or anything, and I wish I could learn a trade, but, hell, I'll get by."

\*

\*    \*

"No, my old man wasn't exactly crippled," Bill from Buffalo says later in the day. We dodge a railroad bull and sneak aboard a westbound accommodation freight just pulling out.

The engine snorts and wheezes. We feel the tie-bar buckle and strain beneath our feet as the train gets under way. Then in a corner nearest the power we squat. Bill continues: "He could walk as straight as anybody most of the time, but in the mornings he used to be all stiff like. He couldn't do any hard work and he couldn't get anything else, and not even that after the big trouble came."

*

\* \*

Happy Joe is a New York Italian with an infectious smile and black shoebutton eyes. He wears a fedora with the sweat band turned down over his ears, when I next see him, and an overcoat several sizes too large which he has tucked up with safety pins in front but which trails along the ground behind like the train of a great lady.

"My kid sister has T. B.," he says suddenly as we watch a scrawny fifteen-year-old turn purple with ineffectual efforts to strangle a cough in a mission on one of the first cold mornings of fall, "and that kid ought to be careful or he might get it too.

"She was never very strong," he continues unprompted, "but that didn't make much difference until Dad lost his job, nobody could get work, and everybody was hard up. Sis wasn't well, and then last summer she worked for five months in a mill. Eleven hours a day. Three dollars a week. She couldn't stand it. All summer she was so white and so thin-like. In September

she began coughing. The company doctor made her
quit. I gave her my room. I slept in the kitchen. We
had to get milk and fruit and eggs and things for her.
Then I lost my job making crates. There was no chance
of getting another one at home. So when I read they
were hiring a lot of new help in Detroit I went there.
And you know what Detroit is like. I stayed there for
a while. Then I just traveled. But if I had any money
I'd send some of it home. Sis is a swell kid."

Practically all the families were hit by the economic
whirlwind. "Else," as Texas explained, "why on the
road?"

Yet even in the days of the boom before the big
trouble came, many homes of the boy tramps were extremely tenuous. Death had taken the father, divorce
the mother; separation divided the family and many
never had had a home at all.

"Tell you the truth about it, Shorty," replies an olive-
skinned Southerner to my question, "I honestly do not
know my real parents. I was born near Nashville, but
I ain't ever seen my father, although he is supposed to
be living in Memphis. He has a wife and three kids
of his own and he isn't any good much. My mother
never kept me. She went away and I was raised by her

sister but never adopted or anything like that. My
mother is married. She lives on a farm up in the mountains. I haven't seen her for almost ten years. I just
sorta drifted from place to place."

* * *

"They say my father is somewhere in Chicago."
Peg-leg Al, who lost his leg between two cars in Texas,
is talking. "But I don't know. As a matter of fact,
I don't know very much about my real father. I lived
near Chi all my life, but that was with my grandparents,
and they died two years ago. My mother never came
to visit us after she left for Pittsburgh when I was a
little baby during the war. Some say my father was a
soldier, others just a man traveling through the country,
but I don't know. I never could find out, and I got so
I didn't care. I stayed at different places near Ham-
mond for about the last two years. Then at Christmas I
scrammed for California. On the way I had some hard
luck in Texas."

Hard luck in Texas! And Al is crippled for life.
His right leg is docked above the knee. He stumps
very efficiently on a self-made peg-leg. The leg apparently pains him not at all, and in a way it is an asset for
it helps him beg.

"I can hit the stem," he says with pardonable pride,
"for a dime anytime anywhere if the cops ain't
glimming."

"I didn't mind living with my mother's sister when my new father wouldn't keep me," Hank, a child of divorce and the depression, is talking as we sit in a mission peeling potatoes as small as marbles and only slightly more edible. "She tried to be nice. But I didn't like my uncle. You know he was always throwing hints—saying how it was hard enough for a man to support his own kids and asking me every day how old I was and then acting surprised when I'd say 'Sixteen' and shaking his head and saying 'Sixteen! God, I was earning my own living when I was twelve!' "

"And that isn't all, Shorty," asserts Vera, a pink-cheeked girl from New Jersey, reaching over and putting her small hand on my coat as we stand in an alley waiting for a cop to pass. "Listen, my mother has had eleven husbands in all. I saw only eight of them. My old man was married nine times. Three of his wives died, but my mother divorced all of her husbands. And if you don't believe me, I hope I die on the spot. I was raised mostly by my grandparents—my mother's folks, that is. Her husbands didn't like me. And she didn't care to have me around either, I guess. Well, there was a younger sister of my mother's at home. And for a fact I know she was married and divorced four times before she was twenty-three. And that isn't all. Wait till you hear this. She had two kids before she was married at all. One when she was fifteen and one when she was sixteen.  And I heard her old man ask her how many kids she was going to have before she got married, and the next day she gets married."

Lady Lou, a very young boy of thirteen and a confessed thief, small, with delicate and refined features, related a most complicated domestic situation, one noon in the kitchen of a mission, as he wiped with a small dish towel the heavy crockery I was washing in water sterilized with creosote.  His real father was married four times; his real mother, six.  The boy liked best—better than his natural parents—his father's third wife and his mother's fourth husband.  Unfortunately for the lad, both these individuals had formed new attachments of their own.  His mother's fourth husband, beginning to take multiple matrimony seriously, had married and divorced twice since leaving the boy's mother.  His mother's sixth husband refused to support the boy.  He had the choice of living with his father's fourth wife who hated and spat at him, of living with his mother's fifth husband, a drunkard in jail half the time, or of taking to the road.  He took to the road.

"I don't remember my real father very much," Dressy remarks to me, one glorious April morning as we sun ourselves on the side of a hill.  He wears a pearl-gray hat which he keeps miraculously clean by wearing a cover made of two red bandanna handkerchiefs when he travels. His coat and pants match. He wears a black slip-over sweater out at both elbows and torn in the back, but with a white shirt laundered every day at a mission or in a jungle, a black bow tie and a pair of black shoes polished daily with crankcase drainings: he is, indeed, Dressy. "He was a soldier. I saw him once in his uniform before he went to France. He did not return. My mother married again about two years after the war. My stepfather had been a soldier, too, but he was a Home Guard and after my father's insurance. I was the only child until the second marriage. Then my mother had three children, two boys and a girl.

"My stepfather never worked very steady. The pension kept us. He was always getting a job and losing it or getting fired or something. He used to get drunk, too. I hated him but I didn't say anything until one day he hit me.

"I was sitting on the porch, studying my geography lesson. When he came staggering up the steps, I pretended I didn't see him. He went around to the back door. I could hear him stumbling in the kitchen. Nobody was at home. All of a sudden he sneaked out on the porch and lammed me. I didn't hear or suspect a thing. Just sock! without warning and my geography flew out of my hand, the chair tipped over, and I was sent spinning across the porch.

"He came at me then. I thought he was going to kill me. I crawled under the swing, and he crouched down to follow. Too drunk to keep his balance, he stepped on the geography and fell. I jumped over him and dashed out of the house. That night I slept in a packing box behind a paper factory. The police took me home. After a big scrap between my mother and my stepfather, everything was all right again, but I never forgot how he looked when he came for me that time.

"Every year he kept drinking more and working less. He used to fight with my mother, but I never saw him sock her until three years ago. It was about nine o'clock. I came in the back door from a movie. When I entered the kitchen there was my mother fighting with him. She was pulling his hair. He slapped her. I saw him slap her. I jumped on him. He shook me loose and grabbed a butcher knife. My mother knocked it out of his hand. I hit him with a heavy iron frying pan right across the face. You could see the blood running from his nose across the soot and grease to the floor. I wanted to have him pinched, but Mother wouldn't stand for it. After a while even, when he didn't come to, she began bawling me out, saying I had no right to hit him so hard. We picks him up and puts him on the bed. My mother was running around crying and washing his face with hot water and blaming me. She always was like that. One day she hated him, next day she was crazy for him."

"After mother died we were all sorry for a long time."
Bust, one of the toughest child tramps I have ever encountered, is talking as we sit in the door of a box car
and let our legs hang out in the sun. Less than two
hours previously I had seen him pound an older transient's face into a red ruin for a fancied insult. Small
but tough, his body had the lithe springiness of a panther
when he moved. Of medium height, broad of chest and
abnormally narrow through the hips, he had the appearance of a triangle standing on its apex, and when he
struck, his arms seemed to shoot in and out of the de-
fenseless man's body with the rapidity and power of a
locomotive drive shaft. The big transient's knees had
buckled at the first of these relentless blows. His head
snapped back at the second. His hands dropped and
his eyes glazed at the third. Then one knee bent, and
he began toppling like a smokestack with a side of the
base removed. Over he went sideways and face down,
the remorseless fists jabbing as he fell.

"And then," Bust is continuing his story, clinching and
unclinching his hands to work the soreness out of them
in the sun, "we got a housekeeper. Father began going
out to dances. We got a lot of different housekeepers.
Finally we got Mamie. She was swell. She used to
play on the floor with the kids and cook us the swellest
turnovers I ever tasted. All of us hoped Dad would
marry Mamie. And Mamie hoped so too, I guess,
because I came home from school and found her talking

very solemn with Dad. That night when I went to the bathroom I heard her crying.

"Next Sunday, Dad brings home a new woman. She was a school-teacher, I didn't like her from the moment I saw her. The first thing she asked me what grade I was in. When I told her, she said, 'Oh!'

"I tried to get along with her though, but I couldn't." Remembered pain stares from his eyes. Remembered wrongs make his voice bitter. "She was always bossing, and always telling me how good her brother was . . ."

"My older brother was always picking on me," explains Boris, a square-jawed Russian lad of seventeen. Small but thick through the trunk, he had the Slav's chronic melancholy and feeling of self-pity. He wore a seaman's white cap and trousers now almost coal-black with soot and dirt, and a short sheepskin, the collar of which he turned up around his ears although it was not cold as we walked along in the night. "He had a job. I didn't. He was always throwing that at me! When we were little he used to beat me. One night about two years ago he came home drunk, sneaked into my room where I was asleep and socked me right in the face. We wrecked the room.

"Always telling me what to do and then peeking to see if I did, that was mother," he says later, as we sit on a car jerking and rattling forward. "And my sister, always telling something or trying to get something on me. I couldn't ever please them."

"Mother never liked me." Spit, a hard-boiled little girl, is talking as we prepare coffee before dawn in order to board a train now making up in the yards. A small fiery-tempered girl with a chronic scowl on her face, in the excitement of telling me of her home, she let the coffee bag burst. Now she skims the grounds with the only utensil available, my pocketknife. "She just hated me, I guess. She used to beat me, and call me names, and chase me out of the house.

"And my kid sister"—even in the semi-darkness I can see the bitterness in her face and feel the sense of wrong in her voice—"got everything from the time she first came. I got nothing, and everything I got I had to share with her. Daddy gave her things, Mother always gave her a bigger piece of pie. Even at Christmas she got more."

The coffee is skimmed. Spit pours my share into a small tomato can and adds a pinch of sugar. Her own she drinks straight. I toss her a hunk of bread which she eats without comment, dunking the cold crust in the warm drink. Down in the yards a whistle blows. It is time we were leaving.

"Did I ever get a licking at home?" Nick, a Dane, repeats my question. "That's all I ever got. The old man would lick me if I did something. The old lady if I didn't. My older brother would take a poke at me just because I was little. The worst one in the bunch was my sister. She is two years older than I am. She never really hurt me, like the rest, but she was always slapping me in the face because she knew I didn't dare strike her back. If I did she'd tell on me, and then the old man would almost kill me.

"The old lady used to beat me up and all us kids." We sit on a rock on the Tippecanoe. My socks, undershirt and shirt are drying on a nearby willow; Nick's overalls and shirt hang alongside. The shade of a grove protects us from the sun. The cool stream washes the dirt and ashes out of our feet. A binder cutting late grain, clatters over the hill. Three Guernseys cool their flanks downstream. In a treetop a crow caws. I listen.

"And Dad, too," he continues, "she was stronger than he, and he was afraid of her from the time when she broke the ironing board on his ribs and he had to go to the hospital. After that he didn't want to come home for a while. Ma went every day to beg him to come home. Then she sent us kids. We used to get a dime just for asking him when he was going to come home. And after a while he came home."

Dot stretches her catlike body in the sun on the side of a hill overlooking a switching yards.

"This is the life," she says. "No old lady bossing me now. One day I was scrubbing the floor and my old lady didn't like the way I was doing it, so she slaps me right in the face with a mop. It didn't hurt, but I got mad and sassed her. She didn't say anything, just waited for a while until I went into my room. Then she followed me. She had a broom handle. I couldn't duck. She beat me until the broom handle broke. Then she lammed me with her hands until she was tired out."

\*
\*   \*

"Pa and Ma were always fighting," another girl told me. "One day Pa came home half drunk and Ma socks him and he socks her back and she got up and kissed him and they both laugh. Then Ma give me fifty cents for ice cream and Susan a dollar for beer and a quarter for steak and we had a celebration. It was the day they were married on."

\*
\*   \*

"Oh! sure we used to have some scraps at home," Hank says as we play checkers in a bumping box car. His face screws up in a vinegary expression as he attempts to check my queen. "But things weren't so bad until the big trouble came. Although," he adds, not unfairly, taking a pawn, "there were always little troubles too."

# III

## WHY DID THEY LEAVE HOME?

HAPPY Joe and I sprawl on some wisps of straw in a box car, waiting for the hour when the eastern manifest freight pulls out. It is late afternoon and raining very hard, a cold autumn drizzle that chills through damp clothes and penetrates thin soles, and arouses a feeling of nostalgia for vanished summer and sadness for the memory of what life might have been. We have had our free bowl of soup and cup of stew at the mission, and an order to leave town before breakfast. The odor of wheat lingering in the wood of the box car revives our unappeased appetite and enhances the loneliness of the day and the misery of a box car in the rain. Why should anybody not a fool or a philosopher be taking the dreary road today?

"Did the old man kick you out?" I ask.

"Well, no." Loyal still to his family, Joe does not want to give the wrong impression. "He didn't exactly kick me out, but he gave me plenty of hints. He hasn't worked steady in the last three years," Joe explains. "There's seven of us kids at home, and I'm the oldest. I'm seventeen. I worked for about six months two years ago for a grocer who gave me no wages but, you know, food and stuff. Then he closed up. I couldn't

get anything. The old man kept giving hints. Last
fall they cut down on our relief. We had to go to bed
because our house was so cold. I cut nine cords of wood
for a man. He gave us two. That wasn't so bad, and
I thought I'd stay until Christmas. I got the kids a duck,
too, for Christmas, but I ain't saying how I got it. Then,
before the old man could start giving any more hints, I
scrams."

\*

\* \*

It is later in the fall now, almost snow time. The
lumber shed, deserted and in decay, divides but does not
stop the cold wind that charges full from the north. Fern
and I listen for a train that is soon to come up the grade.
She wears a boy's sailor blue mackinaw, a boy's cap,
and with two pairs of overalls is not cold. But there was
a thin scum of ice on our jungle water this morning, the
last flight of ducks have gone south, and the wind is
threatening snow. Fern limps a little from a sore ankle
turned two nights ago when she stumbled over a switch,
and with the day and a cold breakfast she is depressed.

"They were always picking on me," she replies in answer to my question. "At home or at school, it made
no difference, everybody always blamed me for everything. Nothing I did ever satisfied anybody. I hated
school worse than home even before the old man went
on charity. I was always given the hard things to do in
school, and at home if there was a dirty job I got it.

"I didn't have any clothes to wear to school. So one day a guy says to me, 'Get wise, sister, get wise.' So I got wise. And the old man catches me taking my first two bits from a fellow and he goes kinda nertz. He calls me down on my knees in the kitchen and Ma comes in and takes my part. 'Why shouldn't she take two bits?' Ma says. 'Somebody in this house has to earn something.' And the old man slams the door and goes out to get drunk. 'Gimme that two bits,' Ma says. 'Gimme that two bits, you dirty slut, before I kill you.' So I says, 'Like hell you will.' And I scrams."

*Why did they leave home?*

The mission waiting room is a swarming ant hill of men who keep pushing in out of the cold and snow. Every available seat is taken. Men and boys crowd the aisles and cover the steps, leaving only a small lane for entrance and egress under the balcony and near the registration desk. Transients squat on knapsacks or stand in discouraged but talkative groups, waiting for the happy moment when stomachs can break their twelve-hour fast on bread and beans. New arrivals appear in the door in a cloud of steam, their snow-covered feet being the first portion of their body discernible as they clump down iron stairs. Outside a Minnesota blizzard howls a wolf-song through deserted snow-banked streets. Snow piles on window sills. Frost creeps over panes. The thermometer, dropping steadily, registers 27 degrees below zero.

Boo Peep and I rest our weary backs against the bricks of an unused fireplace.  He sits on a pack; I on the floor, my heavy sheepskin serving not uncomfortably as a cushion and a shield against the blast of cold air that strikes us as the door opens.  A small thin-framed lad, Boo Peep wears two cloth overcoats, the inner one cut off just below the waist.  My larger bulk and bigger coat protect him somewhat from the draft.  Fourteen hours he spent in a box car.  He is still cold and hungry. A ring of bologna and a loaf of bread washed down with snow has kept him alive for two days, as he came up from the South and East.  The sub-zero weather is not pleasant—particularly when, as in Boo Peep's case, you have no shoes.  An old pair of four-buckle overshoes, miles too big and with several air holes, cover his feet. Two pairs of cotton socks, a pair of worn tennis shoes encased in a layer of newspaper have kept his feet from freezing—he thinks.  Not until later will he know. Although he has been less than an hour in the mission, he seems to be thawing out.  The blue cold is retreating from his face.  He snuffles.  At each snuffle, his whole body rises with the force of the inspiration.  A deep cheek scar half an inch wide and twice that long, memento of a blow earlier in the fall from a railroad watchman, is suspiciously coloring and sore.  Boo Peep is not quite fifteen.

"A guy's crazy to go out on a day like this if he doesn't have to.  Why did you leave home?"

"I couldn't go back to high school in these pants.

What the hell, I'd rather take to the road. The old man? I don't know where he is. I've had four of them. Every one worse than the other. Then, Ma died a year and a half ago. I stayed on with my step-father for a while. He was a barber and he said he'd teach me the trade afternoons, and I could go to high school in the morning. But he took another woman. Naw, he didn't marry her. And she took a dislike to me as soon as she saw me. She gave me the dirt in all directions. They never bought me a pair of socks or gave me a nickel to spend. All I got was a dime from some of my friends for cutting their hair. So when I asked for a new pair of pants after working thirteen hours a day all summer and I didn't get them, I left."

Frank is almost eighteen. He raises his head across the collar of his coat.

"That's like the bastard I worked for," he contributes. "Milk fourteen cows a day, up before daylight and still working in the field when it's dark. And did I get any money after eight months' steady work? I got a pair of old boots with holes in them so big that I couldn't tell where the top was, and an overalls patched until it looked like a crazy quilt and when it got cold last fall they gave me a horse blanket smelling of liniment and manure to sleep under. And I thought, screw you, I'm hitting the road.

"Oh, sure, I got an old man, but he ain't worked in four years, and you know how it is. Four younger kids home. So I thought I'll work for a farmer and earn my board anyway. And did I work! And did I earn my board! So last fall I knew there was no use going home, and I just beat it."

* * *

Pete, a diminutive gnome with a slight limp, joins the discussion. His voice comes excited and asthmatic from a chest covered with fold upon fold of newspaper and clothing.

"Yes, and I'll bet you're glad you beat it. I know I am. Work! Work! 'Why don't you get work?' That's all I hear from the old man for a year. Cripes! What does he expect a kid to do?" The words come out of Pete's mouth bulletlike. "I try a job cleaning a shoe store every morning from four to six o'clock for a buck and a quarter a week. And one morning my mother forgets to wake me. And I'm canned. The old man goes nuts for a while. So finally I asks him, 'Why the hell don't you get work yourself for a change? You ain't done nothing now since the war!' Then he bangs me with a chair, and I lams it."

Pete's voice ends in a shriek. His small deep-set eyes flame indignantly at the memory of injustice. His voice forces itself more and more until it is wheezy and ineffectual as a locomotive losing ground on a grade.

*Why did they leave home?*

Still along the Mississippi River banks the sandstone caves are damp and chill. Three nights ago a hungry boy froze to death within a dozen yards of our cave, while above us a careless city celebrated. But hunger and cold and death ride the green light of every train the child tramp flips. Soon he knows them as old acquaintances. Below us, only a smudge of snow marks the end of winter. Already the Mississippi inches upward on the bridge piers with young freshets. And today a warm sun shines upon our doorway, drawing us out of our caverns as it draws the raccoon out of his hollow tree. It is a day when even the rheumatic old men venture out, the social leaders look up summer sailings, the penned-in worker begins to plan his vacation, and the child tramp starts to itch with a desire to travel which will not be denied. Well-thumbed time-tables are studied, routes compared, and experiences exchanged. By God, if nothing else happens this summer, we're going to see the country.

"Geez, it's two years ago since I left home, and I ain't never wanted to go back yet."

Jud, the hard-boiled, is talking. Elated with a new pair of work rubbers, a zipper-front jacket, and a barber school haircut, he looks upon the world as his oyster.

"No, sir, the old road looks good to me. Square meals don't come every day, but I eat better than I ate at home and no grief about the old man being out of work all the time and how he used to do so much when he was as old as I was, and then the snoopy old social worker coming around asking questions and the cops waiting for a chance to hang something on you. If they do give me a rap now nobody knows about it and if I haven't got a clean shirt there ain't nobody else showing off his new sport roadster."

"That's so for you perhaps, but I'd like to see my sister again." Flaxen-haired Fred is but sixteen.

On the road eight months, he has been living on his own for over two years. Mother dead, father dead, twelve-year-old sister in an orphan asylum in Milwaukee.

Fred's memories of home are pleasant. "Things were slick then. Nothing to do but go to school and play. And every evening after supper we used to gather around the piano while Mother played and we all sang songs in German. But then, I suppose—" His hands rise, his shoulders shrug, in an age-old gesture of resignation and impotence.

And while his voice does not break, in the corners of his blue eyes there gathers a suspicious mistiness. He blows his nose lustily between thumb and forefinger, snorting to distract attention.

I know Fred's story. So do all of us. Home might have been happy for Fred, playing with a younger sister, eating Mother's cookies, attending the circus with Father. But Father died and Mother followed six months later, and this morning as spring creeps over the frost-ribbed hills, Fred is a bum, welcome nowhere, pushed out of one city and into another, on the road because he has no home, no friends and no relatives. Still in his tired eyes shines something of the eternally unconquered Teuton, and the habits of cleanliness his mother taught him keep him neat and tidy on the road, the qualities of courage and honor his father inculcated keep him straight in the midst of a life of shame and dishonor.

*  *  *

"My old man was always mean," an Irish boy from Boston explains, "my stepfather, that is. My real father, I don't hardly remember him. He died a couple of years after coming back from the war. Gas. Everything was oke then. But my mother married about five years ago. My stepfather had two kids. A boy and a girl. The girl was all right, but I never liked the boy, nor the old man neither. I took a poke at the kid the first day he came to our house; I could lick him easy. The old man beat me. I hated him. And did I lick his kid before I left! Two black eyes, a broken ear and a bloody nose . . ."

*  *  *

Kay is fifteen. Her blue eyes, fair hair, and pale cheeks are girlish and delicate. Cinders, wind, and frost have irritated but not toughened that tender skin. Sickly and suffering from chronic undernourishment, she appears to subsist almost entirely upon her finger nails which she gnaws habitually.

"There wasn't"—she takes a finger away from her mouth long enough to join the discussion—"much else for me to do but go. There are eight younger kids at home and one older sister out of work. Dad hasn't worked steady for four years. Sis, for two. Mother got a job scrubbing—$7 a week, and that's all we had to live on except for some clothes we got from a lodge. We wouldn't take charity. So when a farmer offered me a chance to work all summer for potatoes and vegetables for the family last winter I took it. I could have stayed with his wife, but I thought maybe if I skipped around through the country I could earn some cash and send a few bucks home. But it don't look much like it now."

"You'd look fine sending anything home, kid" Helen, a young box-car prostitute, sneers at Kay's threadbare boy's overcoat and holey overshoes. "If I ever get any money, I'll put it here." She pats her abdomen. "I lammed from home because I always wanted to see California. So when Frank says 'Let's go' I went. Wife or no wife could stop me although she did have Frank pinched."

*Why did they leave home?*
It is the middle of September and already a tinge of winter haunts the air in spite of the mellow sun of

autumn and the warmth of early-changing, reddening leaves. Twelve boy tramps and three little girl companions sit in a natural clearing in a woods a hundred yards from a railroad grade fourteen miles south of Chicago. A spring bubbles from the ground in one corner, running away in a tiny stream to the woods. Here the child tramps wash their clothing. Bushes are hung with drying shirts, socks, underwear, and pants. Two boys try to bend a shoe nail with rocks as last and hammer. A Titian-haired girl of fifteen, extremely pretty and extremely thin, sews a patch on the seat of a boy's pants. The boy stands very still on a hummock. The girl sews very business-like, as she turns in the edges of the patch and reënforces the center. A second, blond girl boils coffee and potatoes and directs the barbecuing of a small hog. Except for the disproportionate ratio of boys to girls, the drying clothes and the deshabille of many, the gathering seems very much like a high school wiener roast, or a Sunday school barbecue. Nature has been kind to the farmers, and the farmers, with crops rotting in the fields, have been kind to the child tramps. There is food enough in the jungle to feed forty. Vegetables have been collected by the sack. Cantaloupes and apples stand in a pyramid on the ground. The hog, of course, was not a gift. But, then, he might have been hit by a truck.

Ragged, smiling Texas, merry as usual, is returning with a knapsack full of bread which he has begged up-

town. He recounts his experiences and success gustily
and with the pardonable braggadocio of one who has ac-
complished something.

" . . . and one woman asked me why did I leave
home, and I answers, 'Hard times, lady!' Just like
that. 'Hard times, lady, hard times!'"

His auditors laugh.

And hard times it seems to be, lady.

Three hundred and eighty-seven out of four hundred
and sixty-six boys and girls stated definitely that hard
times drove them away from home.

Yet there were other reasons.

Twenty-six of the remaining seventy-nine were on
the road because of some trouble with a girl.

*
* *

"Her old man come over to our house and began to
raise hell," explains a Byron who had been to Wisconsin U. He is wearing a yellow deep-pile camel's hair
overcoat, now spotted like a leopard skin and a hat at
too odd and rakish an angle for a regular, as we wait
in the falling snow in a bread line. "He thought I
ought to marry her, I suppose. But I couldn't see it
that way, when she was a push-over for every guy in
the fraternity row. So I beats it. Being on the bum
is better than being married anyway—especially to
something like that."

"We were all in it.   Drunk.   And we went to a cottage after the football game," Harvey, a well-dressed high school senior from Michigan is telling me his story as we sit on a pile of lumber in a shed waiting for the rain to abate.   "But it was my old man's cottage, so I got the heat.   Everything would have been all right then, but one of the dumb clucks had to start making coffee about five o'clock in the morning.   Her guy was sick, and she got up to make some coffee.   The kerosene stove exploded and set fire to the place.   We got out but none of us had any clothes on.   One girl was burned pretty bad.

"We had cars, all right, and we could have ducked into them, but the cars were locked and our keys were inside our pants in the cottage.

"Everybody blamed me: all the mothers of all the girls and the school principal and my old man.   So before they got a chance to kick me out of school or anything, I says 'To hell with you!' and I hitch-hikes to Los Angeles."           *

* *

"She was a waitress in Memphis," thin, sensual Merle, who had loved unwisely and too well, explains. He was fond of girls, talked of them continuously and smacked his lips as he talked.   "I worked in the kitchen of the same hotel.   I was reasonable with her. I tried to talk her out of it.   But you couldn't reason with her.   She just kept saying I'd have to marry her and that was all. One day when I came to work I peeked out of the locker room. There she was sitting with another woman, kind of an old maid like who must have been a church worker and a cop. So I never says nothing. I just put back on my hat and coat and sneaks out. The hotel still owes me $4.50."

*  *  *

Twenty-eight were on the road because "they liked to travel."

"Home was all right," declared Ted, a small lad whose dexterous, supple movements reminded me of a young kitten. "I could be in high school today, but I never cared for it. As soon as I was fifteen I got a job away from home, and I never went back since."

*  *  *

"I always wanted to go swimming in the middle of winter," said Flo, an Italian girl from South Chicago. "So when I got a chance to go to Florida, I went. Since then I've been just seeing the country."

*  *  *

Twenty-three were on the road because they hated school.

"I hated to go back to high school." Matt, a peculiarly dyspeptic-looking boy of seventeen is speaking.

The upper half of his face seemed to be at war with the lower half. Each tried to draw away from the other and where they met there was a series of tangles and snarls. He looked upon life with a sneer. "No, my folks could afford it, but I just hated it. You know all those glee clubs and athletes and class presidents who think they are so smart. I hated them and the teachers going around the halls smiling and bowing at them. I hated the whole business."

"Nothing I ever did ever satisfied anybody in school," a girl told me in answer to my questions. "I hated them all, particularly the algebra teacher, and the domestic science and that old stuff."

"All my life I hated school," asserted Omaha Red. "I hated it from the day I started. I used to fight with the teacher, and principal and everybody. The happiest year of my life was when I was thirteen. I ran away from school in the fall just before Thanksgiving. I had a cousin on a ranch in Colorado. I stayed with him herding sheep all winter. When I had to go back home in the spring it was like going to jail. He died that summer or I'd be with him today. I stuck it out as long as I could but I hated school and everything that goes with it."

A few girls may have been lured on the road by wandering lads with infectious smiles, good lines, and well-developed techniques of loving. The majority left home not in company with a boy, but with another girl. And not a few were young couples and sweethearts at home. They ran away for many reasons but chiefly because they were in love.

"We were going to get married anyway as soon as I got older and Charley got a job," declared blue-eyed Luella who couldn't have been over fifteen, as the three of us waited in the shade of a filling station on the Lincoln Highway for a ride west. It was early morning and the heavy caravansaries of freight were cannonading by at a fifty-mile-an-hour clip. As thin as a golf stick and as shapeless, she shivered some as the fog cut through a blue blazer.

"We were going to get married anyway," she repeated, "so what was the use of waiting?"

*

*  *

"The old man caught us necking too heavy on the back porch one night," admitted a shapely little lass. "He said I couldn't see Joe any more unless I married him. Joe says he didn't want to get married just yet 'cause he liked to be free kinda. But he was pretty hot for me too and one day he asks me to scram and we scrammed."

"We both hated high school," asserted a dimple-cheeked girl speaking for her swain. He was uptown hitting the stem for groceries. She sat in the door of a box car and smiled at all the passing men and boys, but waited. "We both hated high school and were crazy about each other."

The remainder of the boys and girls seemed to have no articulated reason. They "just left."

*Why did they leave home?*

"Hard Times, lady, hard times"—plus the difficulties and desires of adolescence and the lure of the open road.

## IV

### HOW THEY TRAVEL

THE young tramps seldom remain a week in any community. Relief policies force them to move. In addition, there is the lure of the road inspiring them with hope of better times just beyond the hills and a nervous "itching foot" for travel *per se*. It was, in truth, impossible for the transient boy or girl to stay anywhere when this study was made. Relief authorities gave a meal and an invitation to move on. No matter how tired he or she was, how willing to work, how weary and disgusted with the road and its aimless wandering, he had to take to it. Police did not trouble transients so long as they kept moving. As soon as they attempted to halt, however, police acted.[1] Jungles were raided, soup and bread lines searched for non-residents, mission lists combed. The child tramp was out again on the road.

On the road the child tramp utilizes almost every form of locomotion known to man. Strange as it may seem, the boys walk as much or more than they ride. Out of twenty-four hours, the average child tramp walks at least eight. He walks, of course, not only

---

[1] This study was made before the new transient law was passed. Conditions may have improved some since.

to travel but to obtain food and money. While hitting the stem and begging meals at back doors, he must walk. He must walk, too, from the yards to the relief stations—often several miles. In small towns, the freights usually stop at water towers or sidings some distance beyond the business section. To board a train, in many cities, the child tramp must walk several miles in or beyond the yards. When he drops from the freight, he must drop off some miles before it reaches town. Walk, walk, walk, the child tramp's existence seems, at times, to be a dreary march never ending. If he travels the highways, at least half his time will be spent walking. If he rides the rails, almost as much time and energy will go into tramping.

"Where have I traveled?" Tow-headed, freckle-faced Bob, a lad of sixteen, was talking as we crouched in the front corner of a gondola for protection against a cold wind. "Fellow, I've traveled to every drag in this country big enough to have a flop house. Last winter I spent in New Orleans. Two years ago it was California. This winter it's going to be Alabama and Georgia. You can't name a main I haven't hit or a road I didn't ride. Right now I'm on my way to Seattle, but I'm not staying there over two or three days."

Not all young tramps on the loose have traveled so far and so long, but many have made quite extensive and interesting itineraries.

"I left home last summer," said Meg, a sexy little lass, as she fluffed her hair and powdered her nose in the shade of a box car. "I thought I was going to California, but I left him in K. C. when I found out he was married. Two boys took me to New Orleans and we had a right smart time last winter. In the spring I went to New York, but I couldn't get along so well with those Easterners. I like"—she rolled her eyes—"Western boys."

*
*    *

"I been away from home four times," Fay said, curling her skinny legs under her as we sat on a huge boulder overlooking Lake Michigan, "and each time I stay a little longer. I been sent home three times and once I just sort of went home by myself to see how the old dump looked."

*
*    *

Many boys and girls have been on the road intermittently. They return home for brief visits only to leave again when they find economic conditions no better.

*
*    *

"Off and on," Warnie, a merry, stout lad of eighteen from Montana, said to me as we hit the houses in Chicago Heights, "I have been on the road four and a half years. I first left home in 1928. Me and another kid, we started throwing erasers at each other just for fun during recess. The principal comes in sudden like, and I lets him have one, without meaning to, right in the mouth. He was mad. 'Get your butt over that desk!' he yells grabbing a ruler. I didn't want to let him flog me, so I ducks around and outside. My father and mother weren't living together, but I was staying with my mother and her folks in Austin, Texas. The old folks were awfully cross, I was afraid to go home. My father was working in Cleveland, Ohio, and I decided to go to him. It took me two and a half weeks to get there. The old man kept me until spring. I went back to my mother's but only for a visit. A rancher offered me a job for the summer. I never went home again, steady, that is. I never give them nothing. They never give me nothing. We get along."

* * *

"In 1931, my first year on the road," explained Walt, "I hit the highways. I had a good front. It was a cinch. I went to all the swell joints in the nation. Maine, Minnesota lakes, and Yellowstone National Park in the summer. In the winter I stayed in Alabama and Florida. It began to get tough last summer. I was run out of all the swell places. In California they sticks me in a camp for three months. Since then I have been staying pretty near Chi and the missions."

The older youths have been away from home longer than the younger. For all ages and all sexes, the young tramps were on the road about fourteen months, when this study was made. Boys and girls under sixteen had been away from home about eight months; boys and girls over sixteen (but under twenty-one) about eighteen.

Fall draws the young tramps south, particularly the first cold days in October and November. Later, in December, many return north, with tales of hostile police, hungry missions, and a work relief policy in Southern cities, in which there is much work and no relief. Transients in the North hole up in jungles or bed down in the missions. Southland trips taper off until spring.

In the spring there is a normal northward movement. This movement is predominantly north and east toward the industrial district where, according to rumor, jobs are to be had. By midsummer the movement is westward to the harvest and orchard fields. Autumn again drives the boys out of the rural districts into cities.

Oddly enough, the movement north and east always seems to be greater than it is south and west. In the first years of the depression California was—and it still is—the magnet for many. "Come to California where life is better," urged advertising writers, and in the first years of the depression the boys and girls came, armies of them. Now California is making every effort to keep out the homeless, and young vagrants find it an unfriendly place.

Whether in the North or in the South, the large metropolises call the boys in winter and the smaller towns and rural villages in summer. The reasons for this seasonal variation are simple enough. In winter the boys must live upon relief or what they can beg on the city streets. They need the shelter of a mission or police station to protect them from storm and cold. In summer every farmer's garden, every henyard, offers a meal of mulligan, and every haystack or grove is a sleeping place.

Yet even in summer the young migrants prefer the rural districts near large cities.

"You never can tell," said Slim Jim to me one day, as we planned a route out of Chicago, "what may happen when you get too far away from a main drag. You may even have to go to work."

"Sure," agreed Bill, "if you are near a main drag and things get tough in the small burgs, you can always return and hit the missions for a meal."

The young tramps seek the cities because cities are their natural habitat. Few farmer boys and girls are on the bum. It is the city youths who have been forced into vagrancy, and they wait around cities for a job. And while waiting in cities they are assured of a minimum amount of relief, and consoled and comforted by the presence of many of their own kind, deriving a pleasant feeling of strength and solidarity from mere numbers, like birds and sheep.

For some reasons unknown, city relief stations as a rule are much more stringent in their attitude toward youthful vagrants than toward older transients. Where an adult is given six meals and two nights' lodging, a boy tramp is given one meal and one night's lodging; a girl tramp is sent to jail. By forcing the youngster out of town, the relief men say they are forcing them to return home. In reality, because the young tramps have no homes, they are forcing them into begging and thieving.

This policy, too, forces them into the smaller cities and semi-rural towns. Here are no tax-supported relief stations, no shower baths, no soup kitchens, but thousands of sympathetic housewives, mothers willing to give handouts and clothes, and farmers who can always spare a few pecks of vegetables. Rural jails are always open for any tramp to find shelter without the formality of registration or the necessity of fumigation.

Some become tired of the same climate and scenery and take a long jump across the continent. The majority remain within five hundred miles of the place they once called home. Within a circle, after several experiments, they lay out a route. From city to city they move, making the rounds of different relief stations and returning to different shops and houses, and panhandling the same towns and streets. Occasionally they fly or are pushed off on a tangent into a new hunt-

ing ground and a new series of towns and relief stations. If the new series is equal or superior to the old,
the youths will follow it; if not, they return to the towns
and places that once fed them.

In the first years of the depression the child tramps
hitch-hiked more than they do today. Then they were
not pests on the highways. Motorists were sympathetic, the stem was not so tough, and boys and girls had
not acquired the habit of traveling in railroad gangs.

Since they began traveling in small groups, the boys
and girls have abandoned the highways and motors for
box cars. On the highways the hitch-hikers were separated. Relatively speaking, they were on highways at
the mercy of police and tourists. In box cars and jungles, boys and girls are able to associate in large gangs
and to protect themselves. Girls in box cars are not
entirely at the mercy of any man on the road whatever
their relations with the boys may be. In event of loneliness or illness, the boys and girls have friends to comfort and care for them. Fear of being alone, fear of being spied on and seized by the first cop who comes along
is absent.

In the railroad yards the boys and girls are, it is true,
under the surveillance of railroad police and officials.
With them they play a game, in which, if both know
the rules, neither loses. The railroad police demand
certain things of the young tramps, such as not breaking
seals on cars. The young tramps demand certain favors
of the officials, permission, for instance, to ride under

cover in empties.  Lately the railroad police, trying to coöperate in the government's attempt to reduce vagrancy through the establishment of transient camps, have been more hard-boiled.  The young riders, in defense, have been forced to use strategy and craft to flip trains.

For the young tramps must utilize the railroads to travel in gangs.

At home, in high school, in colleges boys tend to associate in gangs, clubs and fraternities.  Girls have sororities and clubs.  On the road there is not only this natural gregariousness of youth, but the need for mutual protection.  A hitch-hiker on the highway is alone amongst enemies—the men who work and have money and who are suspicious of travelers who have no money, do not work, and yet live.  On the railroad he is with friends.  Hitch-hikers, too, must be clean and neat.  No motorist stops to pick up a dirty beggar, but the police do.  Box cars carry all classes.  Boys who have only a ragged pair of overalls, a dirty shirt, and decrepit tennis shoes can still travel and live in the jungles.  On the highways somebody will sic the dog on them.

In traveling in box cars the child tramps ordinarily require no techniques.  They merely climb into a box car and wait until the train pulls out.  Some cities and towns and some railroads do not permit the transients to board a train so openly.  The boys and men must sneak on.  In other places the railroad police are inflexible about enforcing the rule that the hoboes must

*A happy old wanderer. He was an atheist and could argue for days on the futility and inconsistency of religion—and argue plausibly, too*

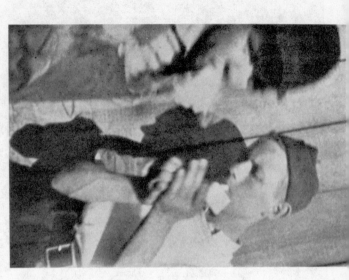

The 15-year-old on the right had been on the road only four months, but was one of the toughest road kids I have seen

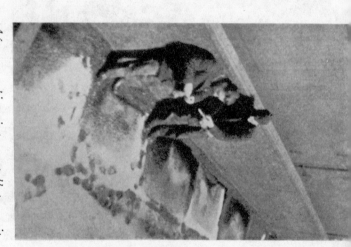

After sneaking into a stall to wait for a passenger, these two stopped to roll one

not board a train until it is in motion. After it is in motion, it is the task of the train crew to keep the transients off—a task obviously impossible. It is not at all unusual to see several hundred men and boys lined up beyond the railroad property fence. A train is being made up a track or two away. The intervening space is patrolled by railroad police.

"Get back there, I tell you, get back," shouts an officer to a pair of boys crossing the tracks.

"Don't let me catch a one of you," warns another as he swings a club in our faces, "putting a foot upon railroad property until that train gets in motion."

The transients are silent. Box cars buckle and bump. A brakie connects the last air hose. From a station near the caboose, the conductor gives the highball. Imperceptibly the train moves as the fireman rings the bell. Like a group of race horses springing the barrier, or football players surging forward when the ball is snapped, the boys and girls surge en masse across the tracks. They alight and swarm all over the train as a cloud of locusts alight and swarm over an orchard. Some climb ladders to the roofs. Others pile into gondolas. The majority choose box-car doors.

And here is one fertile source of the accidents which daily cripple boy and girl tramps for life. The train is in motion. Scores of boys and girls crowd, boost and shove one another. Youths in the car reach down and lift others. Boys on the ground boost friends or try to leap up themselves, and all the time the speed of the train is accelerating.  First you walk, but soon you must trot to keep up with it.  The ones near the door are trying to get in.  The ones away from the door are pushing forward, fearing they may be left.  And in the jumble and confusion, the stumbling over cinders and tripping over ties, someone may fall.  Fortunately the train is moving so slowly that in most cases the youth has time to recover and slide out of the way.  But not always—and another homeless girl is crippled for life, another boy killed.

The railroad police justify their efforts to keep the transients out of the yards by saying that they are not only protecting the companies' property but the youths themselves.  Boys and girls straying between cars and across switching tracks are in danger, it is true, but they are certainly in less danger than when trying to board a moving train.  Inasmuch as they are going to ride anyway, why not let them board the train openly and safely?  Many towns do.

Other towns do not.  Not only do they prevent the transients from boarding a freight before it is moving, but they make every effort to keep the men off after the train has started.  In these towns the child tramps must drop off and board a train far from the yards and often beyond the city limits.  A grade near a block signal is the favorite flipping place.  Here the freights slow up or stop and the boy or girl can, with a little skill and more luck, board the train.

Box cars are the favorite riding place of child tramps,

but they ride anywhere. On tops of cars, between cars, in reefers, in gondolas, on open cars, and in with cattle and stock they ride. I have never seen a boy or a girl riding the rods underneath a car. Deception isn't necessary on freights.

On passenger trains it is. To flip a passenger, a boy must outwit not only the railroad police, but the train crew. The better the train, the more difficult it is to ride, and those attempting to go passenger must separate from their gang. In general they prefer to be with friends rather than travel alone, as they must on passengers. Unlike the adult transient, nervous, irritable, and, when traveling, anxious to get somewhere, the boys and girls are in no hurry. In midwinter crossing the Western plains or the mountains, they may hurry for the protection of cities and the haven of missions and main stems. Ordinarily time is of no consequence, and a local, an accommodation, or a through freight is equally acceptable transportation.

"I don't care how I go as long as I am going," Carl explained one day. "Any place, I think, is going to be better than the last place, but it usually turns out to be worse."

When in a hurry the boys and girls ride passenger. Then, there is an interesting contest between the youth and the officials. The young tramp sneaks into the station somehow and hides somewhere in the stalls near his train. In this hiding place he crouches until the train starts. Then a dart from the covert, a climb into the blind front of the head baggage car, and the boy is riding. Different tactics are used to outwit trainmen. Sometimes the child tramp arrives before the train. At other times he comes running up the stalls just as the train is leaving.

The favorite hitch is the blinds. Yet I have seen a boy dressed in only a suède jacket, reënforced by a layer of newspaper, curl up on a step and ride into a blizzard. Railroad conductors and cooks have told me of other child tramps whom they saved from starving or freezing on the roofs of Pullmans crossing the Rockies where the boys had no protection from the elements and only the most precarious hold near the ventilators to keep them from rolling to death.

## V

## HOW THEY GET FOOD

THE American young tramps, if one may judge by appearances, are not hungry. To a casual observer, they seem in good health and not bad spirits. When you talk to them, however, or listen to their talk, you realize the important part food plays in their lives. Almost one-fourth of all their conversation concerns food. When you live with them, eating at the missions or in the jungles, you understand almost too well why they are so concerned with food.

The young tramps, I repeat, are not starving. But for growing, healthy boys engaged in strenuous outdoor life, the food they eat is shamefully inadequate. Many relief stations serve but two meals a day, others three, and some only one. No station ever serves second helpings and the Oliver who asks for more is expelled before breakfast. Jungle food is better in quality and, if the pickings are good, more generous in quantity, but meals are uncertain. One day the boys may gorge themselves. The next there may not be a slice of bread or a cup of coffee.

Travel interferes with meals. A youth shivers all night in a gondola. Next day he falls asleep on a hillside and sleeps the sleep of exhaustion until dusk. On awakening he is hungry, but where can he get food? The bread lines are closed. The police have, in one of their weekly raids, cleaned out the jungles. At none of the customary places are there friends or food. The youth can beg on the streets, walking miles perhaps before he gets a nickel. A boy can steal, but the chances are that he will be caught. A girl can offer her body, but as likely as not she will find nobody in the market with desire and a dime. The usual course is to remain hungry until breakfast at a mission for a boy, or until breakfast can be begged by a girl. If the boy is very hungry, he may glom a grub from garbage cans.

The breakfast at the mission, if he remains there, is a thin bowl of gruel containing too few vitamines and calories to replace the energy lost on a twenty-four-hour fast. In one day's fast the boy's body has been definitely robbed of much strength. With work and walking, sleeping out of doors, and riding in box cars, it may be a long time before that lost energy can be replaced. Yet, unlike the adult tramp, all the time the boy is growing. He needs enough food not only for the repair and replacement of tissue oxidized in daily activity, but for growth, development, and future use. He does not get it.

Not only does he fail to receive food enough for a growing, healthy boy, but because he is constantly calling upon reserves he is definitely undernourished. The signs of malnutrition may not be so evident to the casual observer. A dozen child tramps in a shower room or swimming hole appear merely a group of lean and lanky boys. But if the observer is critical, he will note the too-prominent ribs, an abdomen too concave, and legs and arms on which the skin, strange phenomenon in the young, is loose and baggy as if there were not enough muscle and flesh underneath. He will notice, too, the tired, hungry eyes, the nervous mannerisms, and the habitual posture of weariness and want.

Communities differ in their systems of caring for all transients. Almost all, however, give one free meal, work for the second meal, a bed on the floor, and eviction before a second or third day.

A boy tramp arriving in any large city walks from the railroad yards to the bread line. The bread line may be a mission, a Salvation Army flop house, or a municipal welfare station, or, literally, a bread line. Some cities have two bread lines; others, only one. The more bread lines, the better for the boy tramp. Rivalry between them forces each to give better service. Meals are varied, privileges and accommodations greater, and sometimes on lucky days it is possible to get food in both. All agencies follow more or less the same procedure. Generally there is some form of confidential exchange, so that the agencies can compare records and information, keep from being imposed upon, and force the young tramps out of the city in two or three days.

As soon as he arrives at the station the boy registers, receiving a slip of identification. Generally the registration is a mere formality to keep a record of the number of transients accommodated.  After the registration, the youth is usually entitled to something.  Some agencies give him a card for the next meal; others, a bowl of soup immediately; still others, merely an opportunity to work for a meal.  Before a second meal is served, however, the young tramp must work two to four hours.  The work is not onerous, but for a tired boy laboring on a bowl of beans or soup it is difficult enough. The soup is invariably—I write from experience—thin, watery, lukewarm, tasteless, and served without even stale bread, and never with soda crackers.  A portion equals about a small cupful.  No second bowl is ever given, no matter how tired and hungry the boy.

Meals vary from city to city, but the two old reliables are stew and beans.  Stew and beans, beans and stew.  Sandwiches are sometimes given instead—usually cheese or peanut butter.  Once a week, perhaps, a boiled vegetable dinner or hash is on the bill.  Bread accompanies the meal.  The bread is almost always bakery returns, stale and unpalatable, or Red Cross flour bread baked by the missions in their own ovens.  Fresh, wholesome, and appetizing, the latter bread is good— but there isn't enough of it.  Other bakery goods, cake or doughnuts for dessert are usually a day if not a week old.  Early in their careers, the boy tramps learn to dunk.  Sundays or holidays, being days of joy and feasting, a dish of prunes or a rice pudding may be served with the doughnuts.

And while some missions in their publicity claim to serve pie, it is sky pie. I have never had any, have never seen any served to other transients, nor have any of the men and boys to whom I have talked ever encountered a mission meal with pie—save one old hobo. He asserts that on Christmas in Chicago in 1911 he received a small piece of mince pie in a mission, but his memory—rapidly failing—cannot recall the place, he is not sure of the time, and it may not have been mince pie after all.

While pie is entirely mythical in a mission meal—so mythical indeed that songs have been written about it, meat seems to have a more tangible although evanescent quality. Meat is something that was served yesterday, or last week, or is to be served next Sunday. For myself, after scores of mission and relief station meals, I must say, so far as the young tramp's meals are concerned, I have tasted it but once—meat loaf in a sandwich. It is true, I have seen meat cooked almost every day at missions and served regularly at meals. The meals, however, were for local homeless men and not for transients. Mission stew served to boy tramps always has in it a hint of meat. There is an inevitable sliver of bone that sticks between your teeth and small diced squares of tripe, but of flesh-and-blood meat, of muscle and sinew, I have tasted none.

A daily joke at all missions is to ask for some beef stew with a little beef in it. The man behind the counter laughs and replies, "All right, brother, but our beef

stew has no beef in it. So if you want the beef you'll
have to take it without the stew," and he hands you an
empty bowl.

The portions are small. At home a healthy youth
could eat three or four. In many stations the food supplies are never equal to the demand. Such a mission is
called a "hungry" mission. The first to come get the
best. The last to come get nothing. The ones arriving
in between get soup thinned with water, stew diluted
with water and potatoes, and something called coffee.

About 4:30 one afternoon as I was working in the
kitchen of a hungry mission, the dining room manager
came in.

"Watch your step tonight," he warned, "the police
are sending over about a hundred new men from the
jungles across the creek. Some are here already and
we'll have to feed a lot of extras."

Unconcernedly, the paunchy cook inspected his supplies. He added a peck of mashed potatoes and four or
five gallons of water to the beans and to the stew, diluted the weak coffee with more water, and called to me.

"Hey, Shorty, cut all those slices of bread and corn
cake in two. Just slice them down the center."

He went to the door of the manager's office. "O. K.,
boss, we take care of them."

And we did. But of the fragments there remained no
five baskets.

Because of the reduced portions served, in time of
necessity, at crowded as well as hungry missions, experi-

enced old bums utilize tricks for stealing food from a boy or an amateur. They try the strategy on the young and comparatively innocent boy tramp traveling alone or on any other unsophisticated fellow they believe will not fight immediately.

With Fred and Boris, I ate in a small mission one night. So crowded was the waiting room that men sat on the floor, lounged against walls and stood in idle, patient groups not unlike cattle waiting for the pasture gates to open. After an hour in line we were squeezed into a small dining hall evilly ventilated and nauseating with the smell of men unfamiliar with bathtubs and un-debauched by the refinements of towels and soap.

Our supper consisted of a bowl of beans, two-thirds water, two slices of bread, two doughnuts very stale, and a cup of dunking coffee—coffee used only for dunk-ing because it has such a vile taste. We muscled in on a bench at a crowded table. I dipped a spoon in my coffee, carefully skimming off the flies.

Sitting across the table from me was a man with the face and features of a gargoyle. Fixedly he stared at the food.

Yellowed, wrinkled, his face was cracked like an old pair of dancing pumps. There was a mad expression in his eyes as though he had seen visions and endured nights of horror. Inured to misery and suffering, never-theless, I experienced a feeling of revulsion that a creature once a man should now be a caricature of one. I removed my spoon from the coffee. The gargoyle,

I noticed, was staring hypnotically at the door behind me. He nudged his companion. "Well—ah-h, what's that coming in the door?" he exclaimed, half-rising and pointing directly over my shoulder.

I turned and looked.

So did my two friends.

Nothing exciting was there. Merely the regular line of men shuffling forward for their soup.

We turned back to the table. Our doughnuts were gone.

At another mission, in another city, I sat at a bench with four men. My meal was a bowl of soup, a cheese sandwich, a piece of corn cake, and a cup of insipid coffee. I raised the coffee to my lips. As I did, the man to my left grabbed the sandwich and the piece of cake with the filthiest hands I have ever seen.

"You don't want them, do you, brother?" he asked, and as he spoke he pawed, crumbling the bread, cheese and cake into a dirty mass. Before I could remove the cup from my mouth and protest, he had spoiled the dinner for which I had worked four long and hard hours.

No crowd at a football game jammed as we jammed fighting our way to the small window where bread— just bread—was issued. Nothing else was given to transients in this city, and the police had a pleasant habit of arresting no bums, but knocking hell out of all who panhandled. The crowd pushed and strained and grunted. Within a cage like a bank teller's was a thin young man and bread, sliced bread. Two slices were given to every man lucky enough to fight or worm his way to the window.

A tall lumberjack received his two pieces, made as though to leave the window, whirled back and darted a hand in past the thin young man to the precious tray of life itself. He seized half a dozen slices of bread and withdrew his booty before the doler of food could stop him. High above his head he waved the booty. Even as he waved it little Boo Peep sprang like a terrier snapping at a bone in the mouth of a Great Dane. One of his small hands held an unopened knife which he rapped smartly against the Swede's wrist. Reflexively, the lumberjack released the bread. Before it reached the floor there were a hundred hands grabbing for it—but Boo Peep came out with two slices.

Whether adult or young tramp, you learn rapidly on the road. You learn to eat at a "hungry" mission with your eyes wary, your attention concentrated on rapidly consuming the small portions of food, and one hand and arm half-circling the plate much as a dog throws a paw protectively around a bone.

For girls there are less accommodations than for boys. Boys can slip in front of a mission for a meal. Girls on the road can appeal to but a few agencies and those agencies are swamped with demands from local cases. Generally they get their food in other ways. And these ways are woman's age-old ways of using her own body and a man's desire to attain her ends. The boys, in the majority of cases, provide the girls with food, even as men in the upper world provide their women with food. The methods by which the boys secure food for themselves and for the girls are begging, stealing, and very rarely indeed, working.

Begging is by far the most common occupation of the young tramps. Even in the country where it is easy to raid a farmer's garden or henyard, begging is more common than stealing. It is easy for a young tramp to beg food. Few back doors refuse a hungry boy bread. If then at a butcher shop he can get a hunk of bologna or a few wieners, he has a meal. Storekeepers, too, are solicited and less frequently restaurateurs. Housewives, especially in the smaller towns, are "hit" regularly and successfully. Bakeries always have some stale returns.

The techniques for ordinary begging are simple. The boys appear at the back door of a bakery or a house—preferably a small, individually owned one—and ask for something to eat.

"A good way," explained Lady Lou—a boy with the complexion of a girl and one of the most successful younger "promoters"—as we stood before a bakeshop, our nostrils tantalized by a yeast-sweet smell, "is to ask for just a little. Hit a guy for a nickel or a couple pennies and he'll give you a dime. Hit him for a dime and he'll give youse the stony stare. I always ask a baker if he has any old half-loaves that he is going to throw away. He pretty near always gives me something good. I even get pie slices that way." Pie, the boy tramp's idea of manna! "Ask a butcher for some old scraps of dog meat and first thing you know he'll be handing you a ring of fresh bologna. I went into a swell joint in Chicago one time and asked the cook if I couldn't clean up the plates that were coming back from a banquet upstairs; you know, the stuff the big guys weren't eating. First thing you know I was having chicken, ice cream, and pie. And before I left I got a buck from a big fat guy."

"Ask a woman in a house if she's got anything left over," said Boris, handing me half a raisin pie he had just received from a woman, "and pretty soon she'll be cooking you a meal. Ask her for a meal and she'll give you the stony stare."

"Another thing you always want to do," advised Happy Joe as he tried to initiate me into the niceties of panhandling in an Iowa town, "is to tell a baker or a woman you got a kid brother down the stem a ways. Then maybe when you are leaving you'll get something to take along. In that way you'll have a nice lunch for later.

"Or," he continued as we munched apples donated by a German grocer, "if it is a bakery you are hitting you can even do better than that. Tell them you got a sick mother and a lot of younger kids at home hungry."

"Before I hit anybody," Texas is describing his methods as we ride a gondola west, "I always ask if there isn't something I can do for a meal or a piece of bread. I ask if I can't cut the grass, clean out the basement, sweep

off the sidewalk.   The chances are she doesn't want to
be bothered having me work and if anything to eat is
handy she will give it to me and say never mind the work.
Sometimes, of course, you have to work, but I don't mind
that so much if I get something for it."

But when a boy is hungry and unable to obtain food
by begging or working he must steal or starve.

To date, stealing has not developed many complicated techniques among the young tramps.   In summer,
the farmer's gardens and orchards are raided regularly.
Chickens, turkeys, ducks, and even small pigs are picked
up when they stray from the farmyard into a grove.
They are run down, snared, or caught in any convenient
fashion with as little noise and fuss as possible.   Seldom,
I suspect, do farmers miss the fowl.   If they are missed,
the farmer most likely blames a skunk or a fox.

Farmer John, it is true, is the most frequent and common victim of the young tramp's thievery, but there are
others.   Bakery trucks parked early in the morning
before stores, vegetable trucks on the way to market
before dawn, all furnish the youthful vagrant with some
of his needed food.   Sidewalk counters and tables inside stores are raided but not often.   Produce trucks
going to market early in the morning are the boy's best
regular supply.   Boys hiding in the culverts at grade
crossings rush out, board the truck and are gone with
an armful of supplies before the driver realizes he is
being raided.

With what they receive at missions, beg at back doors,

Two youngsters boarding a box car of a moving train

Grabbing an iron for a heist

*How many young tramps will end like this man?—homeless and old in a flop house, begging on street corners*

and steal from farmers and others, the young tramps manage to keep alive. Some meals the youths cook in jungles are very good meals indeed. I have eaten barbecued pork that could not have been cooked better by a black in Birmingham, and a stew which was a goulash fit to set before a Hungarian king. At other jungle meals I have eaten potatoes burnt to a cinder, coffee full of sand, ants, and flies, chicken poorly dressed and sourly cooked, and boiled salt fish that tasted like something inexpressibly evil and diseased.

# VI

## HOW THEY GET CLOTHING

THE relief stations for transients in the large cities feed but do not clothe the young tramps. Clothing is for the local homeless, not for the travelers. A boy or girl tramp must be not only in rags but half-naked to obtain a patched and dirty shirt or a worn cap. How difficult it is to obtain clothing nobody who has never tried can know. I have tried. For almost a week in two important cities of this country noted for their large transient populations and their advanced and humane policy of handling transients, I tried to get clothing in return for honest labor and in response to obvious need.

It was in December and very cold. Snow covered the ground. The thermometer had touched zero more than once the preceding night and morning saw its continued descent.

Dressed as a transient, registered and living at the missions, eating and sleeping with the men and boys, working for my soup and bed, taking the compulsory shower and fumigation, I attempted to obtain needed clothing. Without an overcoat beyond a well-worn blazer, buttonless and out at one elbow, with a pair of trousers out at the knee and in the seat, with an old summer cap that

80

had hung for years in a furnace room, with worn tennis shoes covered by patched rubbers, with a pair of unmatched canvas gloves, I attempted to get some clothes through the regular relief agencies and to no avail.

My journey started in a reefer where Boris and I huddled together with three older men transients in the front of the car, the animal heat of our bodies making an ineffectual effort to keep us warm. We have been riding only two hours, but it has been a long cold two hours, and no swaddling of newspapers can keep us warm. Boris wears a sawed-off sheepskin over two old coats, three shirts and two pairs of patched trousers. I wear a long old sheepskin over a collection of rags.

"Today might be a good day to hit the stem for some clothing," he suggests as we leave the yards and make for a mission. "It's cold and people sometimes give you clothes when it's cold. I need shoes."

And he does. But so do I. My feet are covered with four pairs of heavy socks under tennis shoes and old rubbers patched with adhesive tape. A layer of oiled Manila paper between the top two pairs of socks, keeps my feet warm enough, but the tennis shoes and rubbers look cold as an Arctic night.

We leave our sheepskins at the mission and in ten below weather solicit every agency in the city. The missions, the Clothing Center, the Travelers' Aid, the Salvation Army, the Y. M. C. A, and a dozen other smaller agencies are visited with no success. It seems to make little difference what story Boris and I tell them. The answer is invariably No. No clothes for bums. No clothes for boy tramps.

"But we gotta leave in the morning," objects Boris to the thin young college graduate behind the desk in the Clothing Center. "Lots of folks can't stand the cold in a box car and especially me. I'll freeze tonight without a coat. Don't you think so?"

No, the young man does not think so. If it remains below zero we can most likely stay another day or two at the mission. No, we cannot work for clothing. There are more calls from local cases than can be filled. We are bums and we must be on our way.

Nor was our experience unusual. In all my association with adult transients and child tramps I have never known one who received any apparel from any agency —except a girl who appealed to a Travelers' Aid Society for transportation home and whose case was publicized in a drive for clothing.

Nearly all the missions, it is true, supply needles, thread, and patches to repair garments—and that is all. Twice I was asked why I did not repair my old clothing, and at one place the social worker in charge offered me an extra large patch for the seat of my pants.

"The trouble with you, Shorty," explained Happy Joe as I told him of my difficulty, "is you don't go to the right place. Try the Little Sisters of the Poor over near the railroad tracks."

I did.

The sister in charge of the clothing was not in when

I called. The other sisters, however, fed me and made me comfortable in the warmest room I had entered for a week, and assured me that if I waited I could get an overcoat.

A cold that had been coming on from exposure now began to develop rapidly in the warm room. I realized that if I did not have a bath and a good bed within an hour or so I was scheduled for a sick spell. In my underwear was a secret cache of money. Not wishing to explain, I sneaked out of the room and took a trolley downtown. Twenty minutes later a hotel clerk received the surprise of his life. First when a ragged bum entered and asked for a room and bath. Second when he placed five dollars on the counter as a deposit.

It is well perhaps to keep my experience in mind. Unless you have something concrete to judge by it is difficult to realize that the child tramps must get their clothing mainly by begging and stealing. The road is hard on clothes. A few days on the cinders or cement and a pair of shoes are well worn. Clothes slept in, in jungles or box cars, boiled and fumigated at missions, soaked in the rain, soon disintegrate. Rents and tears appear. Patches will not hold. Replacements are needed.

But if the child tramp cannot get clothing by working at agencies, how can he get it? He can beg or steal. He must beg or steal. Begging is the method used most often. The child tramps beg clothing at back doors, on the streets and at second-hand stores. The clothing stores are solicited regularly—without much success, it is true, but with a persistence that is admirable.  Even a second-hand clothing storekeeper may relent at times.  Stormy, cold weather is the best time to hit a storekeeper and the time of day most propitious is early in the morning or late at night.

"See this shirt," Bill said to me one blizzardy day in a Western mission, "I went out in the snow yesterday without any shirt a little before eight and I hit three stores and in the third one the Big Shot gave me this shirt."  An old and paint-stained but still serviceable shirt.

"Flats where a lot of young married people live are the best.  A young married woman is good that way, she'll pretty near always give you an old shirt of her husband's," he said at another time.

"But I like a woman who's kinda old," objected Pete who was mopping the toilet floor.  "A woman, you know, about forty.  And one who lives in a house.  She'll ask a lot of questions but if you spill her the right stuff, she'll gift you.  I got this whole outfit from one."  An outfit four sizes too large for Pete and pleated with safety pins to protect him from the cold.

"Look at me," commanded Blink.  "You never saw me when I didn't have a good front and you never saw me working for anything either.  I wait until after church on Sundays and when I see a woman going home I follow her and hit her for some clothes and lots of times I get a big dinner, and some spiffs too."

"I never try that," admitted a Jewish boy. "I stick to the rabbis and, by God, I can tell a story that'll make any damn rabbi in this country bawl. And if he doesn't give me what I want, he gives me a card where I can get it."

The necessities of road life, however, do not always wait upon the generosity of the stem. And when begging does not bring success, stealing must. The boys are reticent about discussing stealing, but all who have been on the road six months steal some. Many will endure extreme privations and misery before they become thieves, but in the end they, too, bow to necessity. Others boast frankly of their success in heisting.

The most common place for stealing clothes is off a clothesline in a back yard; the best time, immediately after dark. Then a pair of boys may march through an alley without arousing suspicion. Careless housewives in the hustle of dinner preparations have forgotten coats and suits out for an airing. Later they will be remembered, but in the first hour of darkness the clothes sway unguarded on the line. Open garages, too, at this time furnish clothes, and, in the apartment districts, fire escapes and windows. The boys merely sneak into the yard or under the window, snatch the clothes and run. Some have a pole and a hook. The pole is about six feet long and light. Boys carrying it on a street or in an alley arouse no suspicion for the pole looks very much like a javelin or practice spear. A hook, usually a plain fish hook or homemade barb, is fastened to the end.   From an alley the boys can reach through a fence and pull clothes off the line.   Through an open window they can reach across a bed and lift a pair of trousers from a chair.   This method is quite common, not only for those stealing necessary clothes but for that increasing number of young sneak thieves who graduate every month from the ranks of the child tramps.   These boys steal not in order to wear but to pawn clothes or to sell their contents.   Much of their "fishing" is done later at night when the household is asleep and a man leaves his trousers with change or a wallet in a pocket over a chair or a woman leaves her purse on the bureau.

Girls accompany the boys on their excursions.   By their presence they help divert suspicion or, if the boys are caught, the girls help to free them by appealing to their jailers.   Generally boys provide clothing for the girls, but occasionally the girl dresses the boy.

One morning climbing out of a box car, I tore my trousers so that they were unwearable.   Safety pins, nails, thread and needle were useless.   The pants were literally ripped from my body as I jumped from the car.   There were four of us.   Two were in a hurry to catch another train south.   After seeing that I was unhurt and that the third boy was remaining with me, they left.

We were near railroad shops about three miles from the center of a city.   It was a sultry, late-summer day. My deshabille caused me no inconvenience, although the possibility of being picked up by an officer was dis-

turbing.   I decided to remain in a box car in the yards
while Dopey Jack went up town for a pair of pants.   I
gave him forty-five cents and instructions to buy the
first pants he could get.

Jack had a good deal of muscle but no intelligence
beyond enough to understand, "When do we eat?"

He reacted in a morose and sullen manner toward
the world which he could not understand.   As he
pocketed my money and listened to my instructions I
thought he was a little less comprehending than usual.
But he nodded his head in agreement and left on my
errand.

Noon came.   One o'clock.   Two.   Dopey Jack had
been gone five or six hours now.   I was hungry and un-
easy.   Had he skipped with the forty-five cents?   In
spite of his honest face and affection for me, had
covetousness triumphed?   I began to recall the stories
and verse I had read about hobo unfaithfulness.   Men
of the road look first to themselves and next to no one.

Three o'clock came and Jack.   But no pants.   He
carried two quarts of milk, wrapped in newspapers.   A
loaf of rye bread with caraway seeds, a half dozen stale
rolls, five small apples, a ring of bologna, three frank-
furters, a liverwurst and a head of cabbage filled a shop-
per's bag he dumped at my feet.   But no pants.

Silently and sullenly, he returned my forty-five cents.

"But I thought you were going to get me a pair of
pants," I objected.

"That's a hell of a thing to ask a man for," he replied,

"a pair of pants. I couldn't go up to a stranger and ask him for a pair of pants."

"You don't have to ask anybody. Just go into a store and buy one. Up on the stem. You were up on the stem, weren't you?"

"Sure."

"Well, then why didn't you get a pair of pants?"

"Geez, I couldn't ask a stranger for a pair of pants." He began eating.

Too hungry to argue with him, I ate. The milk was cool and sweet, the sausage fresh, the cabbage a good relish. We saved the liverwurst and rolls for supper.

Hunger appeased, I began a long expostulation, trying to convince Jack that a pair of pants was not an indecent purchase but a necessity for me. He replied very little except to mumble that asking a man for pants was a hell of a funny thing to do. After a time he appeared not convinced, it is true, but at least willing to admit that I had to have a pair of pants and that he would get one. He left for the stem.

It was dark when he returned, but lights from switch engines blended with white steam and made the yards light as day. Again Dopey had a supply of food, the forty-five cents, and a pair of pants—with braces attached and a monogrammed handkerchief in the hip pocket. Where, I wanted to know, did he get them. "Well," he informed me, "I got them, didn't I?"

And he had.

One afternoon some months later I was in the com-

munal laundry of a mission washing a shirt which tore
as I washed it.  I had no other.  All the transients
there, both men and boys, were sympathetic.  They
realized my predicament.  In the morning my card at
the mission expired.  I must leave town.  To appeal to
the mission or any other agency, they knew, would be
futile.  And yet, no shirt in the middle of winter!

Transients, considering their means, are generous.
They will share food, clothing, and tobacco.  Most
generous of all are the boys.  Some communal spirit
makes them realize their mutual dependence and the
ideal of one for all and all for one in need prevails.

I needed a shirt.  Nobody present, of course, could
give me one but all discussed methods of getting one.
One youth promised a shirt the first thing in the morning.  But the first thing in the morning I must be on
my way.  Breakfast and good-bye before the cops come
to chase vagrants out of the city.

After much argument it was decided that I was to go
with Candles, Whistler Will, and old Tim who would
show me that evening how to hit a town for a shirt.

Immediately after our stew and doughnuts we left.
The small apartment house district was our first hunt-
ing ground.  Tim, the older and more experienced man,
talked while we stood some distance away and watched,
not unlike a trio of embryonic vacuum cleaner salesmen
watching the canvass of the field trainer.  Tim would
punch the bell.  When a woman answered he would
remove his cap rather awkwardly and say, "Pardon me,

lady, but I wonder if your husband has an old shirt he don't want. My brother just got out of the hospital and he's sick and ain't got no shirt, and it's pretty cold not to have a shirt. And I was wondering if you would have an old one of your husband's you don't want for him"—a wave of his cap indefinitely in my direction.

One kind lady gave me something to eat, another gave me a dime, but a third called the police, and at the end of two hours I still had no shirt. Personally, I should have liked to quit but Tim was as persistent as a man who takes you angling to his favorite lake, on a day when the fish do not bite. We had been making solid blocks of apartment houses, the homes of usually childless couples or women not above making an honest dollar or two.

Now we entered the tenement district, where babies and children were as common as boiled cabbage and 3.2 beer. Tim's tactics changed. No more punching of doorbells and pretty speeches, but stealthy tiptoeing in hallways and peeking through half-opened doors. Tim's pride was aroused. He was going to get me a shirt if he went to jail in the morning.

We entered a dreary tenement building, poorly lighted. Tim reconnoitered.

"Lam around in back," he muttered, sneaking down the stairway. "I think I got something for us."

Between garbage cans and garage we crawled to where Tim had cached a basket of laundry. We raised the cover and fished inside.

Every garment to my hand felt identical.

"Diapers?" questioned Candles, the youngest, who had left eight younger brothers and sisters behind him in Ohio.

"Diapers," agreed Whistler Will the Lithuanian.

"Diapers," admitted Tim sadly.

# VII

NEAR a small jungle between a railroad track and the Mississippi, a gigantic sewer spues a city's filth into the river. Rains and floods have bit deep holes into the gravel and cinder bank, leaving the sewer's mouth projecting like a huge cannon. Along the north side of the sewer young tramps have constructed a rude shelter, ten by fourteen feet. Decked over with tin and utilizing the sewer and river bank as two walls, the lean-to opens on the water and the West. Sacks of burlap filled with straw lie on the ground. A small narrow bunk held erect by limestone rock runs along the sewer wall. Three cedar posts uphold the tin roof which slants at a crazy angle as though at any moment it might lose its precarious hold on the land and slide off into the Mississippi.

To the front and side of the lean-to smudge fires smoke in a foredoomed effort to keep mosquitoes away from six who have just finished supper in the jungle. The day has been swelteringly hot with the intense unallayed heat of "good corn-growing days" in August in Iowa. Not a wisp of air deflects the smudge smoke which arises straight as the flame of a tallow candle toward the unclouded stars. Long since the sun has disappeared behind the cliffs. Supper is over. The tins are cleaned and stacked under the bunk. Every person in the city not detained by work has gone to the beaches.

"No use to pound the pavements tonight," says Slim Jim, a tall, gangling youth from Tennessee. His face is as red and sunburned as a tomato from riding on the roof of a freight all afternoon. "With a face like mine I'd scare 'em, besides they are all out to the lake."

"Why didn't you have sense enough to come down off the roof?" mocked Helen, a slight but cunning lass of fifteen. She has just finished washing her socks and underwear in the river. With only dirty patched trousers on she has difficulty standing close enough to the smudge to keep the mosquitoes away from her white and tender skin. Her small breasts have blue marks on them and a livid sunburnt scar across one shoulder records a rent in her shirt.

"I couldn't," Slim defends himself, long hands and powerful wrists gesturing, "I couldn't. I fell asleep at Willmar, and I didn't wake up until I was damn' near to Minneapolis and then I thought somebody was frying me in a pan."

"Well, you shoulda been in the gondola coming up from Dubuque with me yesterday. That was hot." Fred, a stubby German with red face and fair hair, is speaking. "Was it hot! Cripes! We thought we must be in hell." He pounds a nail in the sole of one shoe with a rock, using another smaller stone as last. "The rubber heels on these shoes, I put them on the iron in the sun and they begin to melt."

"Hot!" Sawbones, an ex-medical student from Chicago, is speaking. "It was so hot when I crossed the desert in June that if you touched any metal with your naked hand, you would have a blister on your hand big as a boil."

"That was the time," says Helen, "when you saw the wolf chasing a rabbit and both was walking, wasn't it?"

The boys laugh. Sawbones opens his mouth to reply. A mosquito lighting on his nose temporarily distracts him. By the time he has the insect annihilated he has forgotten Helen's crack. After a time Helen gives up the battle with mosquitoes and puts on a still damp shirt.

Darkness comes suddenly now. Lights on the city's streets and bridges rim the river like jewels in a diadem. So Babylon of the hanging gardens must have looked at night when—but the boys and the girl are in no mood to appreciate beauty.

Weary with the heat and their own exertions they recline in silence, on sacks and newspapers. Three try to sleep inside the shelter next to the sewer, three on the ground outside. The beds are not too comfortable. Helen, save for a newspaper and her sweater as a head rest, is sleeping on cinders. Fred has only a coat to keep his face out of the gravel. Slim Jim, unable to sleep on his burning face, has a grain door as bed which he shares with Sawbones. Sawbones falls into a deep sleep as if drugged and immediately rolls out onto the cinders. Slim Jim curses a little deliriously from the heat and hardship as he drives a pair of mountain mules through

the cool valleys of Tennessee.   Helen twitches spasmodically and murmurs, "Is it Mother?"

The fire smolders and dies down.   Mosquitoes rally
to the feast.   Sand fleas crawl out of the gravel and onto
the young tramps.   Lice and other miscellaneous vermin
deposited by other tramps attack the sleepers.   But the
sleepers care not.   Nor do they heed any bites or crawling
things until the morning sun strikes Slim Jim's lobster-
red face, and he awakes with a curse.

A quarter of a mile down the railroad tracks thirty-
four boys and girls are waking in another jungle.   Here
are no lean-tos but a growth of willows and cottonwoods
on an old sand bar.   Paths lead in from the railroad
tracks in three directions to a clearing sixty by eighty
sheltered by small trees.   Grass, fed by moisture from
below, grows luxuriantly and high.   Tramped by many
feet and bodies, it still pushes its way up, making a soft
natural bed.   In the center of this clearing a huge smudge
has smoked all night long, watched carefully by pairs of
boys serving turns.

As we continue down the tracks we find other camps.
Some are near the right of way, others a quarter of a
mile removed.   Five or six girls and boys are bunking
here.   Twenty-five or thirty men and women, boys and
girls there.   Any thicket, any grove along the railroad
track may be a burrow for a boy, a moll, or a bum.

Although they would be a welcome relief from the
heat, caves along the river are unoccupied.   The tramps

believe that sleeping in them in summer "will make you cough."

Uptown, migrant youths sleep unconcernedly in city parks side by side with tenement families driven out by the heat. Here is a child tramp pillowed on his knapsack next to a mother and her babe. Over there is a transient girl who has removed her shoes and tied them to her wrist, sleeping peacefully alongside a fat Jewish clothing worker.

Until late fall the young tramps sleep outside, with the sky as their roof and a camp-fire vigil light. There comes a day, however, when mercury in the thermometer drops low, snow covers the ground, and the young tramps must seek shelter. All older transients, too, must find cover, and the boys and girls who have been living in the rural districts during summer and fall gravitate inevitably toward the cities and the main drag. Relief facilities are swamped. New bread lines form. Old ones are extended. Mission annexes spring up. New municipal lodging houses are opened. Still the relief facilities are inadequate. Without enough accommodations for the local homeless men and women, transients must be squeezed in as circumstances dictate. In the squeezing-in process, child tramps are usually squeezed out.

In the second week after Thanksgiving, Peg-leg Al and I leave the yards of a large Mid-Western city and plod through the falling snow toward the mission. It was Al who lost a leg a year ago in Texas. Through some miracle of regeneration, the stump healed rapidly and when four months later he was kicked out of town, he made the peg-leg of which I told you before, threw away his crutch and returned to the road. The leg consists of two two-by-fours nailed together at the bottom and held open by a cross piece at the top. A wad of cloth rests in this niche and on it Al rests his stump. Pieces of canvas and leather hold the leg to Al's thigh. An extra wide strap runs up and over Al's right shoulder. When he hustles, he lifts the shoulder and throws his body sideways.

We are hustling now.

"Aren't you afraid of slipping?" I ask as Peg-leg skips lightly over an automatic switch.

"Naw, I got some new non-skid on the other day, Kelly-Springfield. I got it from a guy in a vulcanizing shop in Racine. As good as new it is, and I can't slip. See, I leave a regular tread mark."

He points to the snow imprint his peg-leg makes in the light of a switchman's shanty.

It is after eleven P. M. when we reach the mission, an unsanitary rookery of two stories near the yards. Lights are dimmed. A ghostly watchman lets us in. We pass through a dirty narrow hall and down some steps to the night desk.

Behind the desk is an elderly derelict who shakes his head at us. "No beds. Guys what ain't on regular relief get no beds." He croaks in a voice ruined by moonshine and radiator alcohol. "But you can pick yourself a place to park." His hand sweeps the room.

It is a large room, eighty by one hundred and fifty, low-ceilinged and outlined rather than lighted by a dozen small-watt bulbs.

Every available space large enough to contain a man's body on the floor is occupied. In the dim light you feel before you see the forms curving away from the desk and entrance aisle. A half-circle ten or fifteen feet in radius is clear. And in all the remainder of the room you cannot see a space large enough to spread a newspaper. Benches follow the walls, pew-like seats stand in the center of the room. On every bench there is a reclining form. Feet to feet, and head to head they sleep. Some have removed shoes. One or two have checked damp overcoats. Here and there a man has opened the belt of his trousers, a boy has thrown off his cap. The majority sleep in their outdoor clothes, caps or hats pulled down over their heads, legs stretched out, faces to the floor.

Fetid air greets us. We catch the pant of the place— the peculiar phenomenon observable in closed stables packed too closely with animals or among men at a mission. It is as though the room itself had a respiratory movement and the breath were pressing against you, unpleasant and nauseating. In. Out. In. Out. In. Out. And you feel a constriction in your chest, a weight on your shoulders, a giddiness in your head.

The illusion passes. The heavy air remains. Peg-leg

and I step gingerly between and over men in the hope that closer inspection may reveal a place to flop. I almost step on blond hair pouring out from under a boy's cap. The sleeper twitches and convulses. Surely no boy ever had a complexion like that. Over the soft baby skin a flush is mounting from the beardless chin to the white forehead. Surely no boy—and then I notice the adolescent curves under the sweater and the delicate hand peeping from a coat sleeve.

Near the girl a gray-haired man snores exhaustedly. His clothes while worn and wrinkled are neat, and his face lined with worry and age has in it still the marks of character. It is very similar to the girl's. Both, I notice, are sharing the same coat as a pillow. Father and daughter perhaps, blown by the winds of misfortune and chance from a home and comfort to a bed on a mission floor.

A drunk tosses alcoholically, disturbing a half dozen sleepers. He jolts a man who bumps against Al's peg-leg, straddling a sleeper. Al drops, barely catching himself from falling on a man. The man wakes up and curses Al whole-heartedly. Another sleeper is disturbed by the curses, sits up suddenly and bumps his head against my knee. It is my turn now to be cursed.

We stumble to the second vacant spot in the room. At the rear, it is not a happy place nor one in which a man might wrap the mantle of his cloak about him and lie down to pleasant dreams.

A door opening directly into a small toilet greets

us.  The stench of chloride of lime and of latrines is nauseating.

Here, if we wish, with the drunks and late arrivals, we may sleep.  Since nine o'clock, the men have been bunking down on the floor and since nine o'clock the men have attempted to avoid proximity to the toilet door. The first to lie down selected a spot on the other side of the room.  Gradually the floor was covered to the middle and beyond.  At our arrival a little semicircle, damp and creosote-stained, is still unoccupied.  Even as we turn to retreat over the sleeping bodies, a new drunk comes stumbling in.  He staggers crazily but effectively toward the open place, then spins on his heel, and without removing the snow from his cap or shoulders he plops down on the floor in an alcoholic stupor.

His precipitate entrance has disturbed many.  A sleeping drunk wakes, and dashes for the toilet.  Al and I hear him retching as we leave.

"Maybe you can find a better place in the dining room or chapel, boys."  The desk man cheerfully points to a stairway.

The dining room is crowded too.  Tables stand on top of tables.  Chairs on tables.  Underneath the tables men sleep.  And on the benches along the walls and on the counters.  The group in the dining room seems younger, cleaner, and more refined.  There is not quite so evil a stench as there is downstairs.  And yet the steamers and stew pots give off a peculiar mission kitchen odor almost as sickening.

We turn our backs on the dining room, cross a hall, and enter the chapel. A similar sight greets us. The chairs and benches are stacked at the rear of the room. Men are sleeping in every available place, including the platform, and the pulpit.

"We could try the top of the piano," suggests Al.

We could, but we don't. Back into the cold we plunge. It is snowing heavier, but the white blanket is a pleasing sight after the depressing mission. A five-minute walk takes us to the central police station. The door man waves boredly toward a hall. We follow it to the police gymnasium. And again every available sleeping place is taken. A plain-clothes man directs us to the cell blocks. Here there is space. We select a spot.

"Wait a minute boys," the voice of a big sergeant halts us. "Did you come in on No. 9?"

"Yes, sir."

The sergeant questions us about other riders on that train, particularly a dark heavy-set man with one queer eye. As he finishes the examination the hourly signal of the police radio station sounds.

"Are you hungry, my lads?"

"Well, sir, we haven't had any supper, if that is what you mean."

"That's it. And in fifteen minutes, they're serving a night lunch at St. —— hospital. After eating, they'll let you sleep there on the floor and give you blankets. Go to the ambulance entrance. Tell them Sergeant Hennessy sent you. Ask for Sister Anastasia."

Seven more blocks we trudge weary but heartened now by the prospects of food. At the ambulance entrance we are let in by a cadaverous orderly and directed to a dining room in the basement. After a meal such as transients seldom have, Sister Anastasia gives us a pillow and a blanket a piece.

"You can have two blankets, boys," she says kindly, "if you will take a warm bath."

Twenty minutes later, after the strange luxury of a warm tub and rub-down, Al and I, deciding to use two blankets as a mattress and two as covers, curl up for a snooze. We awake at seven o'clock in time to shave before breakfast.

Next day Peg-leg goes south on the Rock Island for St. Louis. I go east. On the way I meet Blink, the one-eyed lad, wearing a patch over his vacant socket.

"It gets so damned cold if I don't," he says as we huddle in a corner of a box car creaking through the frozen night. "It gets so damn' cold when the tears roll down and freeze and then the wind gives me a sharp pain in the back of the head deep inside."

He is wearing a red stocking cap upon which rests a black fedora. "No use throwing it away," he explains. "I'll need a hat in the spring and, cripes, it was hard enough to get this one."

Somebody gave him a niggerhead overcoat ten sizes too large, which he has chopped off to the waist creating an odd barrel-like effect. The sleeves are long to protect Blink's hands. They flop down below the bottom of his coat when he walks, making him look like some odd anthropoid creature with spindle legs, an enormous chest, and long chimpanzee arms.

Last night while I slept in the hospital Blink carried the banner, walking the streets until daylight. Tonight in a mission in another city we are fortunate enough to get a bed.

One of the new missions in the country, this agency housed in a new fire-proof building represents the best in transient accommodations. At ten P. M. after chapel we present our ticket and are ushered into the dormitories. Our coats, bundles, and valuables are checked as we enter. We are sent to a fumigation, shower, and laundry room. A bar of soap and a small crash towel is handed to us. We remove our clothes and give them to a man to put into the fumigation chamber. With about thirty more men and boys we are herded into a hot, dry room where the temperature is over ninety as we await our turn at the showers.

"Gosh, but this old heat feels good after a day in a box car," declares Blink.

"You said it," agrees a mulatto. "This is the first time I've been warm since I left L. A. three weeks ago."

The heat caresses our bodies. Tired muscles relax. Stiff joints loosen up. We begin to sweat. How good it feels to be warm. How good it feels to be out of the snow and cold. How good the anticipation of sleeping on a real bed instead of a hard floor.

The hot shower and soap washes dirt and perspiration from our bodies. A twist of the handle and stinging needles of ice drive out the lazy enervation of heat and fill us with vigor and action.

But the towels—the only towels we have are small hand towels too tiny to wipe both ears.

"Use your underwear," counsels Blink. "Use your underwear. I always use my shirt and underwear to dry in. Then I wash 'em, see, and hang 'em in the drier all night. And in the morning when I put 'em on they are nice and warm."

All the experienced men and boys, I see, are following Blink's instructions. I use my shirt and union suit for a towel, later washing them and my socks in one of the laundry tubs.

Our bath over, we cross a hall to the sleeping quarters. For a moment, as I entered the room, I thought the men were sleeping on the floor again. A sea of faces and blanket-covered forms met my eyes. And through this sea men were wading knee-deep it seemed in some dark substance from which the white calves of their legs emerged from time to time as they lay down.

In a room built to accommodate thirty-seven, one hundred and fourteen beds are crowded. So close together are they packed that a man can roll from one bed to another without dropping to the floor. In the only aisles left between every four beds men cannot walk face front but must hop sideways. Wall radiators above the beds throw off heat. A huge ventilating shaft in the middle of the room sucks up foul air. And strange it seems to lie down in close proximity to so many transient men without inhaling that nauseating "mission smell."

Yet many men and boys, so accustomed have they become to the hard floors of box cars, toss and tumble restlessly in clean sheets.

"I can't sleep on this damn' bed," complains a negro boy next to me. "It's too warm and soft."

He slips between the cots, and rolls up in his blanket on the cold cement floor.

Morning reveals that other transients have found the beds too warm. They, too, have slept on the floor.

At six o'clock we are awakened. Our clothes from the fumigator and drier are cooked clean and warm. We are refreshed and able to perform the two hours' work required before breakfast.

But our ticket forces us out of town by noon. We ask, without much hope, for an extension. Our request, along with all others, is denied. We must hit the trail.

And the trail leads over the hill and far away from a railroad water tower eighty miles east.

A well-beaten path shows us the direction to an old unused ice house squatting like a crippled bulldog on the shores of a lake. I have two rings of bologna. Blink has three loaves of bread and a dozen buns.

We enter the ice house from the lake, lifting aside an old ice chute door and stooping very low. Our eyes, accustomed to the white dimensionless glare of snow, cannot focus in the semi-gloom. We see nothing. We hear nothing.  For all we know we may have entered the kingdom of the dead.

In a moment the pupils adjust.  We see a red flash above us and to the right the dim outline of walls rising straight aloft to an immense vault of a roof in the dark and the distance.  The flash I noticed to my right becomes a fissure in a camp stove through which wood flames show.  We go toward it, walking across packed sawdust for a hundred feet.

Now we can make out forms squatting around an oil drum set upon bricks which they have converted into a jumbo stove.  Ten feet of galvanized drain pipe serving as a smokestack and chimney rises straight into the air.  Above it a white wisp of wood smoke seeks the rafters.  Through a hole in the front covered by a piece of sheet iron held in place with an old Ford axle the transients feed wood.  The stove radiates welcome heat.  We warm ourselves.

While warming ourselves, we take note of the surroundings.  A square forty by fifty feet in a corner of the ice house has been leveled and packed hard with the trampings of many feet.  Around this square sawdust rises like a bulwark to a height of four or five feet broken only by the breach through which we entered.  About forty boys and ten girls recline on the bulwark, or sit on their haunches around the stove.

Planks form a platform for the stove which is mounted upon bricks and rocks.  From the wall on both sides ten feet above the floor timbers jut out nearly meeting over the stove and braced in several places by scantling posts imbedded in the floor. These timbers are covered with sheet iron, tin, and lumber which acts as a roof and retains the heat for the youths. On the west side of the clearing a large piece of tin rising from the sawdust bulwark almost meets the roof. The second side is two-thirds open, a few boards and pieces of sheet iron making a fence rather than a wall. Yet on occasion the transients can fill in the holes in the fence and the breach through which we entered and create a closed room.

It is comfortable under the roof. After a few minutes Blink and I retreat from the stove and flop on the sawdust. Supper is prepared by a tall Scandinavian girl. She allows two assistants and that is all. We contribute our food. In return we receive a full meal of stew, sauerkraut, baked potatoes, boiled turnips and a creamed onion sauce. After supper we sit and gab. It is six below zero. Nobody dares venture out. No newcomers arrive. I am selected with Blink and another lad to stand the first watch and see that the fire does not die.

The third member of the watch is a girl of fourteen who has come from Nebraska in nothing but a jumper, a pair of overalls, and a raincoat. She arrived in the ice house six weeks ago and since has not dared to leave for fear of freezing.

The other boys and girls prepare for sleep. Carefully they pull caps over ears, button overcoats, notch up belts, and lie down with their feet to the fire. Blink and I and the girl from Nebraska sit and doze. After an hour or two we are relieved by a new watch. I bed down on a hummock of sawdust with Blink near a strange girl who is breathing heavily with a chest cold.

"Cover your feet with sawdust, Shorty," warns the girl, who has watched with us. "Like this, see." She indicates her own feet, covered to the knees with a foot of dry sawdust. "Then no matter how cold it gets or if the fire goes out, you won't freeze. There was a couple of guys here a week ago on that cold Saturday night. They didn't cover their feet, see, and the fire went out. One of them is in a hospital over town now."

A few nights later I enter another jungle located in a sandstone cave along the Mississippi River. The boys have sheeted the cave front with boards and metal, leaving only a small narrow entrance to one side at the bottom and a slit for smoke at the top. Smoke is coming from the slit now, curling up over an ice ledge and melting the snow. A canvas flap covers the low door. I stoop to my hands and knees and enter.

I rise, and my head is in a cloud of smoke. Temporarily blinded, I cough and choke, stumble forward twenty feet past a log fire at the neck of the cave and enter the vault itself. Here the air is clear and pure. The fire at the front keeps out the cold. Smoke rising to the roof of the forepart of the cave trails along to the slit over the mouth and goes outside. Twenty feet from the entrance there is no smoke or fumes, only clean heat and air and an odd dampness that never seems to leave caves. Twelve boys and two girls are living here.

Though too late for regular supper, I am in time for a cup of coffee, a roll, and an apple offered me by a black-haired girl. I accept, protesting that I have had a meal uptown. The girl shares the food in my lap.

There is a checker tournament in progress. Three homemade checkerboards rest on the floor in the firelight. Six players move the counters with great rapidity and skill while a crowd of twenty kibitz. The boys must move the checkers rapidly. Each player has until his opponent counts ten to decide upon and to complete a move. Failure to make a move means a forfeit. And there are no take backs.

With three different players shouting aloud and a crowd laughing and kibitzing, I marvel that the boys play so well. One boy loses. Another takes his place. The tournament continues for over an hour until a champion is found. He is congratulated and awarded as a prize a large milk can.

"Now you go out and fill it full of snow," orders a girl with a scar on her cheek. "As champion checker player of this jungle you can provide us with washing and shaving water for the morning."

Some boys continue playing checkers. Others argue over games already played and lost in the same way that contract players hold post-mortems. The majority prepare to sleep.

A large billboard on the floor is the chief bed. A half dozen of us flop on it for the night. Smaller billboards and straw-filled sacks are beds for others. The black-

haired girl lies with a thin boy near the fire.  He spreads
his coat on a straw-filled burlap sack.  She pillows her
head on his shoulder.  They kiss and go to sleep.  The
other girl sleeps between two sixteen-year-old boys.  She
lies on her stomach, pillowing her head in the crook of
one elbow.  The boys lie alongside, each throwing a
protective arm across her shoulder.

*  *

Curious it is but true that the farther away from other
human habitations a boy tramp or a hobo jungle is, the
cleaner and more commodious it becomes.  A jungle a
mile from any other dwelling is most likely neat and
tidy.  A jungle within the shadow of a skyscraper is
seldom fit for sewer rats.  Road-wise kids avoid them
when they can.

But tonight, Texas, Boo Peep, and I cannot avoid one.
We have been chased out of a mission where for the
past two nights we have slept on the floor and where
last night some jack roller stole one of Texas' shoes.
With his ears frozen Texas should be going south, but I
will not let him go with only one shoe.  And so we remain in town in spite of hard-boiled cops, a heartless
relief policy, and the necessity of sleeping in a city jungle.

Transients and town drunks pushed out of the mission
live in an old deserted building near a freight yards.

A door from an alley leads to a stairway and down
into a gray, unlighted basement.  Wood and stone parti-
tions once divided the place, but the wood has long since

been burned. Plumbing and lighting fixtures, too, have gone with thieves. Nothing remains but the stone walls and the great beams of wood and columns of stone and cement supporting the floor above. A double pair of broken windows stuffed with rags and repaired with tin let in the only light on a cement floor strewn with rags, newspapers, and human filth.

A vile and ugly place it is indeed, dark and damp, and smelling not so much of men's bodies as of their breaths. And every night throughout the winter fifty to one hundred homeless sleep here. The floor is clammy to a stomach inflamed by no dehorn alcohol. A frosty chill sweats from the walls. In two suits of underwear, three O. D. shirts, a sweater, a blazer, three pairs of pants and a long sheepskin, I shiver. Texas and Boo Peep in half as much clothing must be nearly frozen.

Tougher or wearier than I am, they fall asleep soon after we bunk down. A chill creeps through my clothes, clammy and deathlike. In spite of efforts to drive it away it penetrates my spine, and with the fetid atmosphere a strange bad taste is in my mouth. Large sewer rats scurry across the floor, rustling the newspapers, foraging in the filth. Drunks stagger in, miss the top step in the darkness, and stumble to the bottom. They call and curse at each other, fight, vomit, urinate in the darkness. Some groan. Many hiccup. One sings a ribald ballad, tuneless and wheezy. And by my side a sixteen-year-old boy coughs, continually, without waking. Deep and chesty is the cough. Between coughs

I can hear his labored breathing. A rattle comes from his throat. The rattle becomes deeper, more difficult. Breath wheezes, a pause. And cough, cough, cough, until the tubes are clear, and the boy can breathe again.

He is, I can tell, very ill. The mission, perhaps recognizing incipient pneumonia and wanting to save the city the expense of caring for a patient, ordered him out of town after a night's lodging. At noon he entered, says an old habitué of the place, plopped down and has been unable to get up since.

"What the kid really needs, brother," explains the rasping, venereal voice in the dark, "is a hospital."

Exhausted, after hours I, too, fall asleep. A dirty light, when I awake, is creeping through one half of a rag-stuffed window. And the boy tramp is still coughing. Face flushed with fever, his respirations are short and fast. Heavy-lidded, inflamed eyes are closed. Parched and dry, his lips are slightly open as he struggles for breath.

"I am going to tell a cop." The jungle buzzard who spoke just as I fell asleep last night is looking at the boy with me. "I am going to tell a cop and have him take this kid to the hospital before he croaks even if they pinch the whole damn' works."

And the poor old man not only tells a cop, but he waits in a light topcoat in the cold until a city ambulance takes the boy away.

Necessity forces the child tramp to utilize every hole or covert promising warmth during the winter. While many go South, more remain in the North. Living as they must a fly-by-night existence, they become ill and perhaps die. Whenever they receive a little protection from the cold they sleep. In country towns the jail is always open. In cities there are bridges, lower levels of streets, old buildings, viaducts, tunnels and sewers. For an energetic and resourceful youth there is usually some shelter. Yet more than once in the winter of 1933-34 and in more than one American city a young tramp went to bed outside to sleep the sleep that knows no waking.

# VIII

## THEIR NEW EDUCATION

OUT of the classroom and into life the young tramps have stepped—to begin their real education. Here are no quizzes, no final examinations, no conditions, no make-ups. And the failures go cold and hungry or die.

"You gotta be quick to get by on the road," said little Boo Beep to me one day when I had missed a train. He caught a step but dropped off when he saw I missed, hitting the cinders so hard that his feet plowed through them like the hoofs of a race horse on a soft track. There was laughter in his brown eyes as he returned to me but also disapprobation. After all, life on the road was a man's game and I should be able to play. "You gotta be quick. Damn' quick," he repeated.

And that, I believe, summarizes the new education of the young tramps. "You gotta be quick."

You "gotta be quick" physically. You must be able to move fast and to a purpose in order to duck by the watchman and flip a freight before it leaves you. You must be able to drop off a train on an instant's notice as it enters town, turn and run between cars, before the railroad police catch you. You must be quick to jump on the tailgate of a truck at a crossing, and to toss off some fruit or vegetables before the driver sees you. You must know how to dodge detectives in the city, farmers in the country, and the law all the time. You gotta be quick to get by.

You "gotta be quick" mentally too. You must be able to size up a town by the time you are out of the railroad yards. Some places have hostile bulls, stony-hearted housewives, and stingy citizens. They give you a meal at the mission and the bum's rush if you try to panhandle. Other towns have possibilities. They can be worked for food, money, and clothing. Some railroad yards are as open as the station. You can enter and stray around them unmolested. The switchmen and brakies will even help you to find a train. Others can be entered only upon peril of a club across the shoulders, or a box on the ears.

You "gotta be quick" in your judgments of towns and men. Some drivers will pick up a girl, feed and care for her for five hundred miles, and treat her like a kid sister. Others . . . Some relief stations can be worked for extra lodgings and extra meals; others will kick you out in the morning if you try any sob stuff. It is to your advantage in some missions to stand up for Jesus and accept the Lord. In others, you might as well forget trying to impress the preacher. Out you go before breakfast no matter how vehemently and sincerely you declare your faith in the Bible and in God. On the stem some men may be approached and hit for a dime; others will read you a lecture; and still others will call a cop. Some housewives will believe you if you tell them you did not have anything to eat for three days.  With others you better offer to cut grass or chop wood before asking for anything.  No time to reflect.  No second choices.  You gotta be quick to get by on the road.

"You gotta be quick" epitomizes the new education of the child tramps.  For if you are not quick, you cannot get by on the road.  And those who do not get by do not live.  They fall beneath the wheels of a redball freight on a dark night and the coroner picks them up in pieces.  They succumb to temptation to steal at an unlucky moment and jail swallows them.  You gotta be quick.

You have to be quick and you have to learn too.  And the first lessons the young tramp learns are those of physical strength, muscular control, and dexterity.  Boy, be nimble; boy, be quick.  Boy, look out for the shack's big stick!  Keep your feet when you get off a fast train.  Maintain balance on the careening top of a box car plunging through the black night.  Duck that railroad cop lying in wait for you as the train enters town in the early dawn.

Learn more than nimbleness and dexterity.  Learn control.  Learn to husband your strength, to conquer fatigue, hunger and sleeplessness, to call upon reserves at will and to keep going.  Weary after walking ten miles, you must walk another ten.  Hungry after a day without food, you must go a second day on a biscuit and a third on a cigarette.  Ignore the pains and demands of the body, and keep going, boy, keep going.

And in going you will learn many things. You will learn, for instance, much of the geography of your country and not a little of its historic past.

The first months a young tramp spends on the road are months of education. His adolescent curiosity concerning the appearance of the Rockies, the coast of California, the color of the deep South blacks is satisfied. He learns what a desert looks like, how tall a skyscraper is, and where the Mormons pray. He sees wheat growing in Kansas, apples in Washington, cherries in Indiana, oranges in Florida, and cotton in Texas. And all this is good.

It is quite common to hear boys arguing about a certain crop, a certain industry, a certain city, and to have the argument settled by, "But I know. I was there."

It is more common to find boys remembering the historic spots of our country.

"Gee," Slim Jim said to me as we stripped for a swim in one of Minnesota's ten thousand lakes. "Last time I went swimming was in the Platte right where the covered wagons used to cross. We had a good trip West. I stopped to see the old Comstock mine—you know, where they got all that gold and silver a long time ago— and Death Valley, and the big water tubes at Virginia City where they used to gamble and fight."

"I saw pretty near everything there is to see in the South," Texas told me as we shivered in the shade of the station outhouse one morning. "Lookout Mountain, Shiloh, Sherman's March to the Sea, and the Fountain of Youth where Ponce de Leon landed."

"Was I thrilled by the Grand Canyon and Hollywood!" a girl described her trip West. "I saw where all the movie stars lived in town and I even saw Ann Harding sitting in a car!"

Six months on the road, and the boys and girls lose their fresh outlook and eagerness. Trips across the continent are no longer educational; they are quests for bread. Towns and cities are remembered not for their historic past but for their relief policies, the hostility of their heavy-foots, the number and generosity of their bread lines and the possibilities of the main stem.

"There is a block in Des Moines on the main drag," Boo Peep said to me as we washed our socks in a mission laundry, "where I can always get a dime."

"And you know," he continued as he inspected a hole in a heel which had twice been repaired, "I think I am going there soon. I always like to have a dime on me, some place. Somehow when I got a dime on me I don't feel so much like a bum. And I don't want to be a bum."

With a dime in his pocket the boy tramp feels rich. He will attempt more, dare more, but will seldom spend the dime. Texas went hungry for two days in order to keep from spending his last thirty cents. It was always his boast that he not only had a dime but "more than a quarter," and rather than feel that he was down to his last quarter he went hungry all the way across

Utah and Nevada. No child tramp I ever met was a happy-go-lucky spendthrift. In a second-hand store the average child tramp bargains better than the Levantine trying to sell a quarter pair of shoes.

Ole, a tall Swede from North Dakota, spent three days in Minneapolis haggling over a pair of shoes, finally securing them for thirty cents—a discount of over fifty percent from the price originally asked. "And," he declared proudly as he exhibited them to us in a jungle on Nicollet Island, "I had over a buck in my clothes all the time."

As part of his thrift education the young tramp protects and repairs his clothing. Mornings at missions and in jungles he inspects clothing, repairs shoes, launders.

"You gotta keep up a better front, Shorty," Fred was lecturing me. He kept his clothes almost too clean. At every opportunity he washed his shirt and trousers; every night, if possible, he washed his socks and underwear.

"You gotta watch your front," he repeated as he demonstrated how to iron a shirt collar on a warm rock. "You gotta keep up a front. 'Cause sometimes it's just the little things like that which make you lose out when you hit the stem. Now me, I always carry a little bottle of crankcase drainings along and rub some on my shoes when I work the houses. A woman likes to see a kid neat and clean before asking him into her kitchen. My mother used to make us take off our shoes."

One night I went down to the yards with Ole and

Kate, who were to catch the Burlington front blind for Chicago.  Ole removed his tie and put it in his pocket, turned his coat and cap inside out to protect them from the inevitable soot, pulled the collar of his cleanest shirt down, his outer shirt and coat collar up, and fastened both with a large safety pin.  Kate wore a jumper jacket with a rope sweater, and a cap made out of a flour sack on her head.

"And now let the old teakettle smoke," she said.

While many of the lessons the boy tramp learns are of unquestionable value, others are doubtful, and still others of undeniable harm.

Too much of the seamy side of life warps a boy's, as it does a man's, judgment of values, and on the road the boy tramp sees little else.  Inevitably he acquires the outlook of the older transients, men defeated and rejected by life.  The boys, at first, fight against it.  They travel in gangs and pairs, reënforcing each other's opinions and egos.  "I don't want to be a bum," they reiterate.  "I don't want to be a bum."  And as long as possible they keep their clothes neat and clean.  But there comes a day when they are alone and hungry, and their clothes are ragged and torn, bread lines have just denied them food, relief stations an opportunity to work for clothes.  A man of God at a mission has kicked them into the street.  A brakie has chased them from the yards, a shack struck them with a club.  An old vagrant shares his mulligan with them and they listen.

He tells them that there are other ways of getting

clothes besides working, that a boy or girl is a fool to be honest when honesty does not pay, and that, while virtue may be its own reward, on the road it buys no groceries. And thus begins that part of the young tramp's new education which is wholly bad.

Begging is the first thing they learn. But a few years ago it was almost a profession. Good panhandlers in 1929 made $4 or $5 a day in any city. Today, the best seldom make forty cents. It takes a good tale, a new approach, and Spartan-like fortitude and persistence to get a dime. Sharp wits and nimble feet are needed now to hit the stem in any city. Cops are hostile; the public is hard-boiled; and jails are waiting. Various deceptions are necessary. The child tramp soon learns all of them.

The most common trick is to fake a deformity. Slim Jim was double-jointed. He could slip a knee or throw a limb out of normal position at will. Taller than I, on an instant's notice he would drop below my shoulders, his legs dangling grotesquely at almost right angles from the knees. His shoulders would stoop, his mouth sag open, his jaw drop, while his face assumed the expression of a crippled half-wit.

Bill had a cane and a pair of dark glasses. In towns he became a blind beggar, tapping along with a stick. Tall and thin, he would suck in his cheeks and stick out his shoulder blades in a deformed stoop as he tapped his halting way along the street. With his extreme youth— he was only sixteen—he presented an appeal which would net him fifty cents in any town.  He never tried to make over fifty cents at one time.  When he had made his limit for the day he quit.  It was, he said, bad luck to be hoggish.

*  *  *

"Now the way to hit the stem," Fred explained to me one night as we tramped the streets of his home town, Milwaukee, in search of prospects, "is to scare them a little.  You want to surprise them so they haven't time to say no.  A guy isn't thinking of nothing and suddenly you are there at his elbow and saying, 'give me a couple of nickels for a cup of coffee.'  He shells out before he can think about it."

*  *  *

"Fast and hard you want to hit the stem," Boo Peep expounded another day as we cogitated means and methods of getting a meal in Rockford, "no use arguing. You ask them for a nickel, and you either get it or you don't.  What you want to do is to size them up, see. Look them over first, but don't let them see you; they get ready for you and say no.  But if you hit them fast-like, the chances are they shell out."

*  *  *

"I used to tell them a long story," Vera said to me, and her child's face already was lined with sophistication and age, "about my mother being sick and how I was walking home, but that don't go now, leastwise on the streets. In houses it is still good but you just waste your breath on the stem. Hit them for a nickel or a dime. Tell them you want something to eat and if that don't go, nothing will."

*   *   *

"Hit the cars," advised another girl when I told her I couldn't pick up any money on the streets. "Hit the cars. If there's a parked car and a woman alone in it, she'll pretty near always give you something. If there is a man in it, stay away."

*   *   *

"I always carry a newspaper rolled up like a club," said Leth, a hillbilly from Kentucky. "It scares them. In a dark street once I made two slugs in fifteen minutes that way."

The lad had come out of the hills two years ago without a shirt, and as he was proud of saying, "I got two shirts now. No more working in the coal fields for me." Short for the son of a mountain man, he was curiously deformed, his left shoulder blade bulging out under his shirt like the comb of a chicken. His hazel eyes had in them a hurt look as though life had defeated him. Yet there was present stubbornness, and obstinacy too, the forlorn stubbornness of a horse pulling on a mountain road a load he knows he can never get to the top.

How to beg is only a part of panhandling. You must

know of whom to beg and where. Old ladies are very generous; women, that is, old enough to have adolescent grandchildren. Unfortunately, they practically never frequent the transient quarter of a city. In the shopping center, well-policed in mid-afternoon, the techniques used ordinarily are useless. The young tramp needs a front better than he usually has. And he must surprise but not frighten the lady—the surprise consisting in the fact that such a neat-looking fellow would ask for a dime. A favorite trick is to inquire for directions. Another is to ask her if she knows anybody who wants a lawn cut or a basement cleaned out. Once conversation is started and friendliness established, the touch is made.

Generous, too, when they have it, are prostitutes, young girls, and married women of thirty. Single women of forty rarely give a young tramp a nickel. Negroes, particularly black women, and immigrants of all ages are generous.

"I never asked a black woman for anything yet that I didn't get," declared Joe, a heavy-jowled Bohunk from the Pennsylvania coal fields.

"Pick out a working stiff with poor clothes when you're going to hit somebody," advised Boo Peep one evening as we discussed means and methods of raising the price of a sack of Bull Durham. "And it's all the better if he's young." Boo Peep was just fifteen. "He likes you to think he has a dime.

"Catholic priests are good; if they think you are a Catholic, they'll never turn you down," continued the expert boy panhandler. "Protestant ministers are stingy. But the Jews never give a cent. You know there ain't much to the idea that gangsters are generous. I never got a dime off one unless he was with a frail. And rich guys will never shell out. I says to one the other night when it was raining in front of a swell club, and he was getting out of a big Packard, 'Mister, will you give me a dime for a cup of coffee, I'm hungry?' And he says, 'If you're hungry why don't you get yourself something to eat?' "

"Fat, well-dressed men have been hit so often and so hard since the depression that they are becoming tough," explained Skinny Joe, the coal heaver. "Poorly dressed men with a grouch and a mean look are often the best prospects because they don't get hit so much."

* <br>*   *

"I don't know how it is out here in the West," a girl from New York said, "but back East a good rule is never hit a Jew, Armenian, or a Chink. When you tell one of those gaffers you are hungry, they don't feel sorry. They feel glad, and try to make you for a dime. Another thing you want to look out for is farmers. They'll talk to you and ask you how you came to be on

the road and where your mother is and all them things.
Then they'll leave you without a cent."

\*    \*

Street begging is only part of the boy tramp's game.
You hit the stem, but you also hit the houses. And
house-to-house begging is an art in itself.

"Look for a yard with a lot of kids' playthings in it,"
coached a youngster from Schenectady, who five years
ago was playing with toys himself. "And a place where
they keep the grass cut in front. Grass out in front,
play-toys in the back yard. You're sure to get something if it is only a meal.

"A good day to hit a house is when there is a lot of
washing on the line," he continued. "You're sure the
woman is at home and got something ready to eat. Also
you can tell pretty much what kind of a place it is just
by the clothes. If there are a lot of men's clothes she
is a good cook. Hit her for something to eat. If the
line is full of women's clothes she is a poor cook and
you better ask for a dime."

\*    \*

"If she asks you in the house to eat," counseled Fred,
who had been asked in often, "always wipe your feet
on the stoop; don't say much at first. Take off your hat
and act scared, kind of. Wait until you've finished eating and she is sitting down and looking at you. Then
she asks you something and you answer polite-like.

Then she asks you something else and you begin to tell a story. If she is a fat woman and sitting down you can tell her anything. Pretty soon she will be bawling and you can have the house."

*  *  *

"Stormy days like today are best," said Don as we bucked a sleet storm one morning. "You always find people at home, and they feel kind of sorry for you being out in the cold."

*  *  *

Not every child tramp is just a street beggar. Many have already graduated to the rank of specialists. The most common and most numerous are "trailers," boys and girls who follow attractions, such as circuses, carnivals, fairs, conventions, and revival meetings that draw crowds. These young tramps trail behind the show and when the crowd gathers they panhandle. And when panhandling is poor, the trailers may turn pickpockets or sneak thieves.

For when the young tramps find begging difficult and unremunerative, they steal. The stealing, to be sure, is not highway robbery. It is chiefly sneak thievery and not regarded as crime at all by the boys or girls. Filching a pie out of a bakery truck, a watermelon off a fruit stand, or a chicken from a farmyard is in their eyes not criminal, but a normal part of everyday life. It is impossible to ascertain how many or how much young tramps steal. Successful burglars or even good thieves are not reduced to living as low as they live. Thieves out of jail maintain a better front, a higher standard of living.

An essential part of stem hitting is the study of men. An essential part of sneak thievery is the study of dogs. On marauding expeditions and even while walking peaceably along the road, young tramps are frequently set upon by dogs which seem to recognize young as well as old vagrants as the natural enemies of their masters' property.

"Terriers and little house dogs are the worst," asserted Ben, a cross-eyed youngster from Kansas, after I had noticed a canine scar as we swam. Unprepossessing in appearance with his cross eyes and badly acned face, Ben could not hit the stem. Men turned away from him in scorn when he begged. Starve or steal, and Ben stole. "Those little short-haired devils sneak up and snap at you when you aren't looking, and do they hurt."

"They're not as bad as police dogs," argued Ralph from his position on the other side of the jungle coffee fire.

"Police dogs. Phooey! Police dogs are all bluff. I never met anybody who got bit by a police dog. They'll knock you down if you run from them, but if you just walk off slowly, they'll leave you alone."

"But not collies," said a black boy from Oklahoma as he dried a freshly washed shirt, "as soon as you turn

your back at one he dives for you.   And does he slash!
I got a pants torn into strings once in Ohio."

"Bulldogs are bad, too," agreed Ralph, "one got me
by the coat one day and I couldn't make him let go."

"I'm not a bit scared of bulldogs," said Ben, who knew
his dogs.   "Bulldogs can't run.   They have no wind.   A
little sprint and they are all tuckered out.   I always
sprint for about a hundred feet then I slow up so Mr.
Bulldog will follow away from the house.   I sort of encourage him on until we get to a rock bed, then it's Mr.
Bulldog's time to sprint."

While the necessities of life are forcing many young
tramps to beg and steal or to starve, many clever ones
are doing neither.   They are learning rackets.   A racket
in the child tramp's parlance is merely a legal method
of making a living under pressure.   It may be a personal
talent that can be exploited.   More often it is something
that can be sold or traded for board and meals.

"I got a racket, see," Mickey explained to me, opening
his knapsack at a mission.   He was dried-up little lad,
thin and undernourished, with the body of a gnome and
the India rubber face of an old man.   Whatever home
he once knew had been broken up for years, and since
1929 he has been on the road.   His eyebrows went up
and his forehead wrinkled as he searched in a bundle
for his racket.   He pawed around with thin talons of
hands.

Out of his knapsack came a thousand soap wrappers, plain squares of white and Nile-green water-wave paper upon which was stamped in purple letters "Wonder Soap" and underneath in smaller letters "For all Purposes." Larger red letters across the middle of the wrapper screamed "Sold for the benefit of the Unemployed."

"Now what I do, see," he continued, holding out a wrapper for me to inspect, "is when I get in a town, I find a soap factory or wholesale house. Then I buy a couple hundred small bars of soap—a whole boxful for two or three dollars, if I got that much, wrap them in these, get a fancy basket uptown, and go out selling."

"How much do you make on them?" I asked.

"I never pay more than three for a nickel, and I try to get them for a penny a piece, or less. I sell three for a dime or a nickel straight. I paid $4 for two thousand wrappers. I sold some to a friend; but just by myself I sold nine hundred bars of soap in the last two months. Mostly I sell to houses. I tell a woman if she comes to the door it is good for shampoos. If a man comes I tell him he can shave with the soap."

"Every town is soft for me," boasted another youth as our train slowed up in the yards of Indianapolis and we prepared to jump. "Watch me hit this one for a meal in ten minutes. Come along, and I'll get you one too," he offered.

I came. My friend entered the first saloon we encountered after we left the switching yards.

"Listen," he said to the proprietor. "I am an artist. I can draw any kind of picture on your window you want. Let me clean off that old stuff and draw something new. All it will cost you is a couple of forty-cent dinners."

The proprietor agreed, reserving the right to reject the work. We cleaned the windows. My friend went to work. He drew a picture of a foaming stein, a fat German, a dachshund, and a Gibson girl, in five minutes. We got the dinners.

"You see, Shorty," he bragged and not without justice, "you gotta have a racket. Then it is a snap."

There are many other boy-tramp rackets. All offer the public some service or entertainment. A Polish boy from Cleveland was an "escape artist."

"I can pick up a living any place there is a fire engine house," he described, taking a short rope out of his pocket. "I just tell them I bet they can't tie me so I can't get loose in ten minutes and I always win. When that don't go so well I try sleight-of-hand tricks in a night club or saloon. I even got a fire-eating act I can put on sometimes. But I don't try that until everything goes phooey. I burnt my lips pretty bad last spring in Denver."

Not all young tramps have honest rackets. One girl I knew bought a small basket of assorted vegetables. With this on her arm she went from house to house. Of a woman coming to the back door, she asked prices so high that she never sold anything. She did not intend to sell anything.  Her racket was to find a back door open—and the woman not at home.

In a jungle one afternoon a girl tramp preparing dinner cursed us roundly for not having a butcher knife large enough to carve the small hog she had roasted.

"Knives!  Butcher knives?" a new arrival asked.  "I got a butcher knife."  He opened his knapsack and out fell two dozen knives.  "Take your pick."

His racket was to solicit knives to be sharpened through a house-to-house canvass, then take the knives to a fence and sell them.

Of rackets, of dogs, of men, of housewives, the young tramps are learning much—and of boys and girls too.

# IX

ON the road now boys in great numbers and girls in lesser ones are learning about life—and who can learn about life and ignore sex?

Opportunities for natural contacts have been rare, but they are becoming fairly common as more and more girls follow their brothers on the bum. About one child tramp in twenty is a girl. Never does a freight pull out of a large city without carrying some girls, disguised usually in overalls or army breeches, but just as certainly and just as appallingly homeless as the boys.

Misery brings the two together. The winds of misfortune and want which drove them on the road create a bond which, while tenuous even as their lives, nevertheless is a bond.

Generally, young couples traveling in box cars find the road an open and a friendly one. Train crews permit them to ride when refusing others. Housewives, remembering the tale of the Babes in the Wood, feed them and give them clothes. Storekeepers find it difficult to resist their appeal. Even the men on the road help. And while the boy and girl pose as brother and sister on the main stem they live as man and wife in the jungle.

133

Brick and Vi are such a couple.  They met on the
lower level of a city street under the loading platform
of a warehouse.  Steam from freight engines kept them
from freezing as they clung to each other for mutual
warmth.  In the morning a fireman shared his lunch
with them.

"And we just sort of paired up it seems," Vi explains.

Henry and Jo are another two who found love and
the wanderlust can live together.  In the yards of Toledo one dark night, Henry, attempting to escape from
a railroad bull, skirted a box car and ran headlong into
someone.

"And wham!  I lets him have one right on the kisser.
He goes down, but he grabs me.  We start wrestling.
I'm winning all right when I find out I'm wrestling
with a girl.  I give her the sign 'Where to, bo?' and
she says 'Up Omaha way.'  So I boosts her into an empty
and we lay there just breathing.  Pretty soon she comes
to and says 'That was a good slug' and I says 'No other
dame on the rods could stand up under it.'  And we
became friends."

Before I met Ray," Little Allie apologized for her
faithfulness as she sewed a patch on an elbow of my coat
one morning, "I was like all other girls."  It was chilly
in the jungle and we sat near the fire.  Last night Ray

had not returned from the stem. Allie, instead of sleeping with some other lad, went uptown, searched until she found him drunk and bruised in an alley, and carried and dragged him home. He slept alcoholically and Allie watched.

"In fact," she continued, "I was a little bit worse. Any man would do, so long as he knew what it was all about. But as soon as I met Ray, I felt different. Since then I just can't seem to get hot and bothered about anybody else."

\*   \*   \*

But not all romance ends happily on the road.

"For two weeks," Blanche, a sad-eyed little girl from Arkansas, told me one afternoon as we stood in the mouth of a sandstone cave and watched the summer rain clean box cars and railroad tracks, "we did everything for each other. He seemed crazy about me. And then one day he just sort of left. I met him a couple times after and he just says 'Hello.' I ask him, 'Did I do anything wrong?' And he says 'No, you're all right.' But he never pals with me any more."

\*   \*   \*

"I met a swell frail in Tucson," Nick said one day as we watched a boy and girl in khaki and O. D. shirts walk up the cinders. "We went all the way to California together and back to Denver and then she leaves me flat."

They called him Kalamazoo Kid, but he was the rein-carnation of Casanova.  We sat before a pine fire which sputtered oddly in a jungle on the banks of the Brule as resin knots fumed and flamed.  Eighteen weary boys stretched out to sleep on the green hillside while hordes of Wisconsin mosquitoes swarmed to the feast.  Alone of the boys, the Kid kept me company by the fire.  He rolled his fifth consecutive cigarette nonchalantly be-tween thumb and forefinger and the conversation turned, as conversations between men so often will, to girls who do and girls who don't.  The Kid had met chiefly girls who do.

"Was that," I asked him, "before you left home?"

"Hell, no," he objected, "I been on the road almost three years, and I was *dumb* as they make 'em before I scrammed.

"Speaking of being dumb.  Geez, I met a girl who was dumb about a year ago in Ohio.  Geez," he shook his head and smiled.  "She was dumb.  Just fourteen and she didn't know where babies come from or nothing. She lived next door to the tailor shop in the little burg where I worked.  I had a bed in the back.  After a while I got her trained so she used to come into the place where I slept.  We used to take off all our clothes . . .

"Geez, it was fun.

"But one night her old man followed her, see.  I didn't know nothing about it.  The first thing I know, bing, a flashlight on both of us.  And there we were, and I didn't know nothing about it.  She yelled and I ducked. Lam, I gets it on the shoulder. The old man hits me with a fork handle. And lam, but I ain't there next time, and she gets it right across the bare seat. I grabbed my pants, shirt and shoes and jumped right through the window, screen and all. We was near the railroad tracks, and I never stopped to put my breeches on, or anything, until I was about a mile down the cinders and my feet were bleeding.

"Good thing I didn't stop, too. I could hear her yelling bloody murder and the old man knocking hell out of her, as I ran.

"I walks to the next town and lucky there's a freight coming in and I hails it for Chicago. About five o'clock next day, I'm high-tailing up State Street feeling kinda light in the head, and socko, I'm in the gutter.

"A cop picks me up, but I can't tell him what's the matter. He takes me to the station, and I got a broken collar bone.

"That was a swell time for me. I stops six weeks in the hospital and I had all I wanted to eat and a clean bed to sleep in and new clothes. Boy, that was swell. The night nurse used to come into the ward every night and look at my chart. And I'd pretend I was going to the toilet. And we'd go down into the linen closet.

"But they kicked me out. I asked them for a job as orderly, but they kicked me out."

"Weren't you ever afraid, Kid," I asked, pushing a pine knot into the embers, "that you'd get some girl into trouble?"

"I never have any bother, I just tell them I had mumps."

"Tell them you had mumps?"

"Sure. Didn't you ever try it? It works every time. I tell them I had mumps and they couldn't get a baby from me if they tried."

"And," I inquired innocently, as I slapped a mosquito on my right ankle, "have you had a bad case of mumps?"

"Hell, no! But that's their hard luck."

Many tell stories of other girls who loved neither wisely nor well, and demonstrate the fickleness as well as the affection of boys and girls.

While no white boy admitted sex relations with a colored girl, all the black boys, seventeen, boasted of relations with white girls or women. Three Filipinos said that they had been very successful with women on the Coast.

"Me?" repeated a youth small even for a Filipino. "I always get a white. No trouble at all. Big blondes. Red-heads—they are the easiest, but it makes no difference. I take them all."

"And did I have it nice in the winter of 1930," smiled Ras, an Arkansas colored boy with ashen scars on his face and neck, "I met a little creole girl in Kansas City who had a bungalow and a bank book, and all I had to do was eat chicken and satisfy her.

"But you gotta be careful of some women or you'll get burned. I got a little bit singed myself once, but a doctor in Memphis cured me."

His face looked ugly for a moment. The scars stood out like dead trees on a burnt-over hill. But the mood passed and he was the carefree lover again.

"You gotta be careful," he repeated and a smile broke through the storm clouds of unfortunate memories, "but you can have a lot of fun with the girls if just one little thing is right."

\* \* \*

Of late there has been an increasing number of maverick girl tramps. They follow the boys, living in the jungles and box cars, serving as mistresses and maids, sharing the joys and dividing the sorrows of life on the road. Generally they travel in pairs. They have no individual preferences and treat all boys and men alike. They wash clothes, sew on buttons, patch pants, cook and tidy up the places where both sleep. Here they are as supreme as old-fashioned housewives in the kitchen. They boss the boys shrewishly, ordering one to hit the stem for some coffee, another to get some meat, and a third to get a new shirt and "for God's sake, can that whistle." The boys obey and serve willingly in hopes of praise and in fear of censure.

No sex rivalry exists between the girls or the boys. The girls are available to any and all boys in the camp including adults and late arrivals. There are enough boys to divide. Occasionally, a pair of girls attach themselves to a gang of boys and travel for weeks in peace and friendship. Other girls prefer variety. They go from jungle to jungle and from box car to box car without discrimination. Any place where there are men or boys, they know they will be welcome. They enter a box car or a jungle—and without more ado the line forms to the right.

One afternoon in September, near a city in the grain belt, two of these girls entered a jungle where thirty or forty men were cooking mulligans. The girls very efficiently helped out with the meal, washed tins, and tidied camp. Then they made a proposition. There was a box car on the tracks near by. They would go there and the men, in pairs, could follow. If a man had money, a nickel or a dime would be appreciated because one of the girls needed shoes. If not, the man could come anyway, but in lieu of cash, he must help prepare the girls' supper which they declared should be ready by six o'clock. All afternoon the girls received the men and boys in the box car. Some men doubled back on the line and repeated. Others visited both girls. Promptly at six o'clock the girls quit, demanded their supper, divided the seventy cents in cash, and caught a night freight for the East.

The girls on the road are young, as young or younger than the boys. All girls I have seen with the boy tramps were under twenty. Older women vagabonds travel the roads, too, living with older men.

On a freight pulling South one night a skinny little girl of sixteen with dishwater eyes and matted fair hair left the company of three boys in a reefer, who were perhaps a little slow, for a box car of older and more vigorous males. All night she entertained them. At a water stop, other men, having heard the good news, rushed forward to the car. By morning every man on the train knew who and what was in the Chesapeake and Ohio car next to the load of lumber. Two of us, fearing the child might be murdered, complained to the brakie. In the cold light of early dawn he went to the car and demanded the girl. She came to the door a little bit drunk and very undressed. Heartily she cursed the brakie for his Good Samaritan deed.

"You big fat fool," she called him, "you Y.M.C.A. dummy. Why do you have to spoil it all? Why can't you let a girl alone when she isn't hurting you? Everything was fine, all right, and now you've spoiled it all."

The brakie made her ride in a car by herself. From the door of this car, however, she talked to the men on top. At the first opportunity she dropped from the train —and two dozen men followed her.

Girls there are on the road, but not enough, and the boys and men denied natural sex outlets turn to other and less approved ones—chiefly to masturbation or to perversion. In any one-sex group homosexuality may appear. Among transients there are few of the inhibitions that tend to check it among others. It is impossible to estimate the extent of perversion among men on the road today. But, as one of the boy tramps told me, whenever you see a trainload of transients, there is always a wolf on the tender and a fruiter on the green light. Like the vultures following a caravan, the perverts trail boys, waiting with bribes and force to ensnare them.

One of the first lessons that a boy learns on the road is to beware of certain older men. These men become friendly with a lonely boy and attempt to seduce him. It is to protect themselves from the approaches of such men, as well as for other reasons, that boys travel in pairs or gangs. In addition they offer mutual protection although they belong to rival gangs at missions, relief stations and in jungles. A man attempting to seduce a boy is set upon and trounced severely by any gang of boy tramps that comes along.

One day in a jungle I encountered a man who was so bruised and battered he could scarcely stand. Both his eyes were closed, a cut two inches long gashed one side of his forehead. His nose was squashed. All of his upper teeth were missing. His breath smelled of dehorn alcohol. Believing him to be the victim of a drunken fight of the previous night, I made him comfortable and went for some water. As I passed a box car, a half-dozen boys stopped me, asking me not to do anything for the wolf. Two nights before, in a gloomy part of the yards he had enticed a boy into a box car. The lad, while small, was muscular and well able to defend himself. He escaped to return next day with the first gang he could muster. I had seen their work.

Tales of wolves using wiles and force to gain the body of a boy are as common as college widow stories around a campus. The older man befriends a boy, giving him food or clothing. He tries to gain his will by persuasion. When persuasion does not succeed, he attempts force. He lures the boy to a deserted corner of a freight yard where the boy's screams cannot be heard, or some night at a lonely water tower he induces him to drop from a train, or he gets the boy drunk and takes him into a thicket.

At times the wiles succeed. I have seen wolves and their little "lambs" or "fairies," and their relationship seemed to be one of mutual satisfaction. The man and boy were pals. The older man got clothes and food for the boy, later teaching the boy how to get both for himself. Far from being miserable, the boy did not want to be separated from his friend. He resented and refused all efforts at his "rescue."

In a mission older men give boys some bananas, candy, or tobacco, and take them into the toilet or a dark corner and love them up. One day I saw a long-nosed man sit next to a boy to whom he had given a pair of shoes the previous evening. His hand strayed over the boy's body.

The boy got up, saying loud enough to be heard in all the room: "Mister, I don't like that sin. I mean I don't like it. And you can have back your goddam shoes if that is why you gave them to me."

# X

## RELIGIOUS LIFE

CASUAL association with the child tramps indicates that they have no more religious life than a healthy young colt. For them, it seems, sufficient is the evil or good of a day. If they have enough to eat and a place to sleep they are satisfied. Continued contact, however, over a period of weeks and months modifies this first impression and reveals a religious and spiritual life of strange intensity. Not that the boys hold Sunday school spontaneously, or build Druid altars in the woods. Nor do they, as the mission preachers are always urging, accept the Lord.

But if religion is a search for values, the boys are religious. There is in their lives a vague quest for something beyond the present, a hope of union with the beautiful and the good, with the purpose and cause of life. This religion, indefinite and unexpressed, is a potent influence in directing the boys at present, and it will be more important in controlling them in the future.

There is, of course, the religious atmosphere of the majority of the relief agencies which shelter and feed them. The purpose of the missions and of the Salvation Army is frankly religious. Before the depression these were the only agencies which considered the problem of the homeless man. Since the depression they have expanded their work from that of rescuing human souls to that of feeding human bodies, but the religious background of their work remains. Every mission has its "No Case is too Hopeless for Jesus" and "When did You Last Write to Mother?" signs, and various Biblical quotations chalked on blackboards at strategic points. Services are held daily. Often meals are furnished only to men or boys present at the services, and many a boy with hunger stalking him becomes a "Pork Chop Christian." "Convert and feed" was the motto of missions years ago. Today it is "Feed and Convert," but in the eyes of the men running the missions the conversion still is the most important work.

\* \*
\*

We sang:

> "I need Jesus, I need Jesus.
> Every day along the way
> Yes, I need Jesus."

The long-haired preacher strained at a voice which had in it neither tone nor resonance.

His fat face became pink, then red, and finally an apoplectic purple as with a sweep of a hymn book used as a baton he brought the song to a close. "Now let us try that chorus over again, boys," he says. "Wait a minute until you get the tune."

A woman, dried and sexless, played on a piano without tune a hymn without beauty or melody. We returned to the song. The preacher's arms pounded the air with the heavy strokes of a woodsman chopping a tree. I need Jesus. I need Jesus. I need Jesus. This time he paused for breath before the end of the final chorus, and let us falter rumblingly to a close.

"That's right." His hands slapped together. "Everybody here needs Jesus."

"And a new pair of pants," added Texas, sotto voce, his curly head bending in my direction, a mischievous smile in his twinkling blue eyes. The shadow of crafty lines disappeared from around his mouth, and Texas was a kid again attending Sunday school in the Lone Star State. But that smell of mission men, that torn coat, the disheveled hair, the frost-bitten ears belonged in no Sunday school. Down if not damned as the preacher implied, we sang on, going through the routine of conforming to a creed many of us neither believed nor respected; we were singing for beds.

"Let us stand now in prayer," says the preacher. We stood and bowed our heads while he talked with the Lord about us.

Tired bodies ease back into chairs and eyes begin to doze. The preacher pours a glass of water. He puts spectacles on the end of his nose and thumbs a Bible.

"For the blind shall see," he reads, "and the lame shall leap."

At the last word he leaps into the air and clicks both heels together.

We open our eyes, lean forward. Again he reads the verse. Again at the word "leap" he leaps into the air, clicks both heels together and comes smartly down upon the platform. He shouts. He waves his hands. He pounds the rostrum.

Sermons at missions are skillfully designed to attract and to convince the homeless male. Their very defects, their rambling incoherence, lack of unity, overemphasis, stressing of inconsequential detail, banal humor and tangent qualities in which one idea suggests a second and a third until the central point is lost amid a babble of confusion, fit in very well with the psychology of their auditors. So do the stereotype illustrations and the references to contemporary events as proving the infallibility of the Bible. The transient mind has limitations. It must be approached circuitously, and the men at the missions are masters of the indirect religious approach.

They are not, however, very familiar with the psychology of the young tramps. Accustomed to the adult down-and-outer, the old, boozy, lazy, and often mentally incompetent, homeless man of ten years ago, the mission men fail to comprehend the difference between them and the new young tramps. For one thing, the boys have more education, more sophistication. They are not to be convinced by the homely arguments sufficient for the older man in days past. Ten chances to one the man was suffering from a hangover. His alcohol-befuddled brain clouded every stimulus, refracted every impression. A preacher merely by shouting at the right time may have been able to "reach" him.  Today's boy tramps cannot be converted so easily.  They know more facts, more history, more politics and economics.  When the preacher tries to account for unemployment as being the will of God, they do not believe him.

Nor do they believe him when he relies upon stereotype sentimental pictures of home and mother to convince his congregation of a point.  Five or ten years ago, the mission preacher could appeal to the wandering boy to return to his sorrowing mother and his aging father. Today, the wandering boy knows he will help his parents more by remaining away than by returning.

He has no background of sinful experience and dissipation to which the preacher may appeal as justification for his present need.  None of his money was squandered upon harlots and riotous living.  Unlike the older man, he knows little of gambling joints and houses of booze and sin.  Nor of bonanza wages and foolish sprees.

For him life has merely been progressively difficult as month after month, at home, he saw more worried lines on his mother's face, less bread on the table and increasing distress in the house.  To appeal to him to quit sinning is foolish.  He has, in its larger aspects, never sinned.  And because he has never sinned, he cannot blame his past misdeeds for his present misery.  Without this self-accusation, religious conversion of the kind attempted in missions is difficult.

Some youths in spite of all effort fall asleep.  Ned, a brown-eyed Irish Catholic from Frisco, keeps objecting

to the theology.    At last he can stand the ideas of the
minister no longer.    He gets up and goes out to vomit,
although he knows that he will be forced to carry the
banner all night in streets stung by sleet which sends little
electric shocks through your face as it strikes.    Neither
my theology nor Texas' is strong enough to drive us out
into the cold.    We fear only the time when, services over,
we'll have to leave this warm room for a bed on the tile
floor downstairs.

Tonight is testimonial night.    The preacher calls on
the Lord to witness and on us to declare our faith in
Jesus.

A man rises, a short ratty little runt with a wart on
the end of his nose and a nervous tic.    He twitches his
shoulders and speaks in a voice that is falsetto and
eunuchal.

"I ain't ashamed to tell what Jesus done for me.    He's
done more for me than anybody else.    And I ain't
ashamed to say what he's done for me."

"There you are," waves the minister, "that's what
Jesus does for you."

A boy tramp, scared stiff, new to the road and lonely,
rises down in front, his red hair standing up like bristles
on a wire brush, and, unable to say anything, he blushes
beet-red.    His mumbles are lost in the confusion that
seizes him as he realizes that all eyes are on him.

"Never mind, Jack," the preacher is kind and encouraging.    "And if you can't say it, we know how you

feel anyway. There it is, that's the way Jesus makes you feel. Good all over. Even if you can't express it."

A filthy old drunk, full of dehorn moon and evil odors, pops erect like a Jack-in-the-box, and, like a Jack-in-the-box, now that he is erect he does not know what to do about it. He sways. His bleared eyes stare uncomprehendingly around the room. He slobbers.

"What did I get up for?" he asks. "What tin da worl' I get up for?"

And he sits down.

Over in the corner near the door, a gigantic Scandinavian lumberjack wearing a red plaid mackinaw unfolds himself slowly like a carpenter's rule. He unhinges to a height of six feet six, raises a hairy fist as large as the bole of an oak tree, glares at us belligerently and asks, "What did Jesus do for me? I will tell he did a lot for me. Once when I was cruising in Washington he saved me from putting my foot in a wolf trap. I was cruising along marking trees, and suddenly I go to put my foot down and I stop because I hear somebody say: 'No, Lars. Don't do it.' I look down and there was a wolf trap. And Jesus he save me from putting my foot in it."

His companion, a smaller Scandinavian, gets up before the giant sits down. He begins, cutting in on the preacher's remarks: "What did Jesus do for me? Jesus has done everything for me. Who gave me this cap I have on? The Lord gave me this cap. Who gave me the coat I have on? The Lord gave me the coat I have

on. Who gave to me the shoes I have on? The Lord
gave to me the shoes I have on. What, I ask you, did
the devil ever give to me? What did the devil ever give
to me?"

"Nothing," says the giant who has been looking at
and listening intently to his companion. "Nothing. To
hell with him."

Nobody laughs. The preacher goes on. The converts
confess. We stand and sing "Brighten the Corner Where
You Are." The services are over.

Through a narrow hallway we pass in single file and
down a rickety flight of steps to the low-ceilinged transient room. In one corner is a desk behind which sits a
bald dyspeptic with a face like a balloon from which the
air has been released. He is to give out beds if any are
given. The men and boys mill around in front of his
desk like cattle at a dry water hole.

A little window in the wall behind and above us opens.
Our friend in Jesus, the preacher, sticks his nose through.
"No beds," he shouts, "for out-of-town men." And the
window slams shut.

The mummy at the desk reveals a ghoul-like anima-
tion. "No beds," he chortles. "No beds, you guys.
Bunk on your ears or get out."

Get out into the storm. Not Texas and I. We bunk
on the floor, spreading newspapers, for the cement is
rough and leaves an imprint in our skin.

"They talk about Jesus," says Blink bitterly, for he
has no newspapers and his clothes are wet, and sleeping

on the rough floor, while not a new experience, is not inviting, "but I ask one of them gaffers for a bed for my sick buddy in Chi. I says to him, I says, 'Listen, mister, the kid is sick. He ain't been able to eat nothing since we left Denver. Look at his face! Look at his eyes. Can't you see they are glassy like? Can't you see he's sick? I'll let you take my coat for a bed'—and I had a good one then—'while I go down and hit the stem all night until I bring you back the lousy fifteen cents.' And he says, 'Nothing doing, fifteen cents cash, flop on the floor, or carry the banner.' And we flops. Next morning the cops kick us out before breakfast. And they takes buddy from the train in Cinci cause he's too sick to do anything but gurgle-like. And they feed him on the black bottle because he ain't got no friends."

"Ain't it the truth?" agrees Nick. "It's Jesus this and Jesus that, but on your way, bum, tomorrow. Listen, I'm going to tell you something. Listen, you never saw a fat guy eating at Sally's and you never saw a skinny guy playing the drum. How do those Christers get so fat if it ain't off our lean shanks."

"Why do they always have to yell at us?" asks Fred, as he spreads a clean tarpaulin taken out of a clean knapsack, on the floor over clean newspapers. "It doesn't take any guts to yell at us. Why doesn't he say something to the big boys, the bankers and things?"

"He says plenty to the big boys." Happy Joe looks dark and serious as he inspects a crack in the upper of his shoe.

"He does not." Stolid Fred for once is inclined to argue.

"He says plenty," Joe repeats unconcernedly. "He says 'gimme' and when they give he says 'thanks.' "

Wizened little Pete, looking more like a gnome than ever, does not join in the sardonic laughter. Unable to sleep on the cold floor without "gettin' pains in the head," he sits erect on a bench, and draws his head deeper into the folds of his always too large overcoat until his nose, resting on the collar, seems the only prop that keeps him from disappearing entirely. Yet still his voice squeaks angrily as it comes muffled from the depths.

"And that's why every mission has a sign saying 'it's never too late for Jesus'—but it's always too late for beds."

Slowly his nose creeps below the rim of his coat collar. Only his eyes remain, more inflamed, more somber than ever. Then they, too, close.

Two days later, Happy Joe returns from hitting the houses to our cave jungle, full of good cheer and Dago Red. Earlier in the day we stole a hog and for the first time in weeks were comparatively warm and well fed. Bust has a bottle of dehorn. More drinks. Texas sings, "When the Work's All Done This Fall." We all sniffle. "When down the boy did fall, and he won't see his mother when the work's all done this fall," and join in the last lines with spirit. Then Texas sings a more realistic cowboy ballad concerning the sentimental and sodomistic relations of a boy cowboy and a heifer.

Happy Joe rises to his unsteady feet.  The dehorn
on top of Dago Red has made him drunk but friendly.
His face flushes a deeper maroon under its customary
coatings of soot and dirt.  His black eyes glisten, and
his voice is a little blurred at first as he sings.

> "I don't care if it rains or freezes
> I'll be safe in the arms of Jesus.
> I can lose my shirt and britches,
> He'll still love us sons of bitches."

We all join in the ribald chorus.

> "Am I Jesus' little lamb
> Yes, you goddam right I am."

"Who give to me the pants I got on?" he mimics
the mission convert.  "The Lord give to me the pants
I got on.  The Lord give to me—the Lord, hell."
Storm clouds cross his face.  Ugly lightning flashes
from his eyes.  Only a little opposition now, and Joe
would be ready for a fight with fists or knives.  But
nobody opposed.  "The Lord, hell," he repeated, "I
stole these pants in Chi."

And yet, in all fairness, I admit another side to the
mission.  It is true that the preachers do not understand the boys very well.  It is true that the missions
too often kick the transients into the streets and out of
town.  Still, many preachers make a sincere effort to aid
the boy tramps.  They extend the boy's sojourn from
a few days to a week.  They try to get clothes for him

and to make him comfortable. When he must leave town, they give him a note to the next mission and as soon as possible find him a job or a home where he can work for his board.

It may be the religious influence of the mission; it may be a projection of themselves; it may be a deep longing in the human spirit; whatever it is, many of the boys believe sincerely, although unorthodoxly, in God.

"God," says Texas unexpectedly, late one night as we sneak through a farmer's grove dark as the bottom-less pit, "is guts."

For half a mile along the tracks the grove runs somber and dark as the black forests of Thuringia. We stumble through it, tripping over bramble, crashing into bushes, stepping on dry sticks that crack like pistol shots in the quiet air. Branches of trees lash out at us, stinging our unprotected faces, for our arms are full of food. Texas carries two chickens, their necks neatly wrung. My arms are heaped with cantaloupes and vegetables.

"God is guts," Texas repeats half an hour later in the jungle The chickens, cleaned and spitted, are already taking on an appetizing brown hue above the blaze. Potatoes and field corn roast in the coals. Coffee simmers. A green streak of dawn circles the east. Morning is greeting us fresh and keen in a pine-scented country, and breakfast, too, is greeting us in a country where a man needs breakfast to keep going.

"Yes," says Texas, as he turns one fowl, "there is a

God and that god is guts. What makes a guy keep pushing on, doing things when he's all in, walking when he is so tired he can sleep standing up, going without food when he is hungry? It is his guts, ain't it? And when a man loses his guts, he's lost everything. Anybody can get by in this world if he just keeps his guts. He can lose his money, he can lose his friends, he can lose his front, and he can lose his health, but if he keeps his guts he ain't lost everything yet. But if he loses his guts, he's all washed up. There ain't nothing left. Because when he loses his guts he's lost his god, and then he's no better than a stick or a rock, or anything else. For it's his guts that make man different from everything else, and so long as he keeps them he doesn't have to care if he's hungry or cold or down and out. His god and his guts will see him through."

"But when he dies, Texas, where does he go then?"

"When he dies," says Texas, eyeing approvingly the brown of a chicken's drumstick, "he goes out like a match."

Nor are orthodox conversions absent among the younger transients.

Pearl diving in a mission kitchen is a sour and smelly job. There is little soap and much lysol. The worker's drain boards are permanently rancid with stew, water, and garbage. I was glad to leave washing dishes and to accept the more difficult task of cleaning ventilators in the kitchen.

The lad assigned to work with me and to boss me was twenty-one, but he looked older. His shoulders had the resigned stoop of an old man. On his brow was a corrugation of wrinkles which he kept continually in motion by a nervous tic so that they undulated like waves. Self-pity and weakness were in the lines of his mouth, yet determination too, and in his odd green eyes was the light of a zealot.

"Thank God," he says as he scrapes grease off the blades of a ventilating fan, "I got hungry."

I look at him uncomprehending, wondering what point the joke will have.

"Thank God," he repeats, "I got hungry and entered a mission in Chi. . . .

"You know," he continues, and pride and disillusionment fight for dominance in his voice. "I went to Wisconsin for three years. For three years," and now disillusionment and bitterness conquer, "I learned nothing but lies and bunk from those godless men, telling us there was no God, no evil, and that you should go out and do it with any girl who was willing.

"I went there because my sister and my mother wanted me to be a college graduate. They were paying my way. But I quit last January. And I got a job in Milwaukee. I lost my job in April, but I didn't want to go home after a scrap with Ma and Sis over my school. I went to Duluth and then to Minot but I couldn't get a job. A trainload of stock was coming East. I rode to Chi. In a couple days I was flat broke. I slept two nights in Grant Park and one night under the *Daily News.* Next day I didn't have a thing to eat. That night I walked up Madison Street and entered a mission.

"I sat down because I was tired and listened to the preacher. In three minutes I learned more than I learned in three years at the 'U.' I learned that life was worth living, that truth, goodness, and chastity were actualities and not just words, and that love is something we share not with the beasts but with God.

"And that night I had a vision." The corrugations in his forehead now are twitching rapidly like waves in a troubled sea. His eyes glitter. His hands tremble and shake. His voice chokes with emotion "Like St. Paul on the road to Damascus, I had a vision and my whole life changed." We continue cleaning ventilators.

Little Alf is thirteen. With his supple, jointless movements he reminds me, more than anything else, of a thin alley kitten. We are cleaning the floor of a mission. We push broad brooms ahead of us, disarrange chairs, and clean out the débris. An odor not of sanctity but of unwashed bodies lingers after the six o'clock services, as we finish our task. Using his broom as a vaulting pole, Alf clears a row of chairs. We climb a flight of uneven steps to the dining room where the one meal a day is given to transients in return for two hours' work.

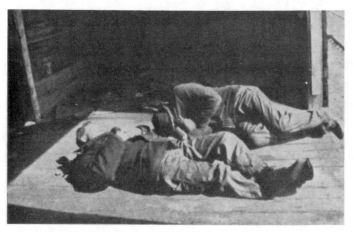

*Basking in the sun on the floor of a box car*

*"I wonder if the shack saw us." Having boarded a redball, two youthful transients looked to see if the coast was clear before crawling on top. Notice bindle, evidence of an amateur bum*

*Home of Moonshine Joe, who had a punk of about 16 he had taken from a freight*

*Jungle-cave between the river and the railroads: three youthful transients lived all winter in the tent and from 10 to 20 occupied the cave*

It consists of sawdust soup, a hunk of moldy rye bread, and a doughnut "so stale," says little Alf, "that you could play horseshoes with it." Not even a cup of dishwater coffee to dunk your doughnut. You bite bravely and pray God your teeth don't chip or gnaw like a dog chewing infinitesimal quantities of meat from a bone. After supper we can sleep on a dirty wooden floor and get slivers in our faces—or scram.

We scram.

It is raining as we stumble through the yards in the August twilight and climb into an empty box car. The northbound red ball is not leaving for four hours, but we breathe more freely and feel a sense of joyousness just to be out of the mission.

In the growing darkness we speak softly. The rain increases. It is no longer a gentle patter but a steady drone changing to a torrent as wind sweeps the drops against the sides of the car.

Out of the water and blackness comes another bo, a girl.

"Where to, boes?" Her voice trembles childishly.

"Up Iowa," answers Little Alf.

I scratch a match with my thumbnail to light a cigarette and inspect our companion.

She is younger than Alf. Hatless, coatless, in short knickers, she looks like a little tomboy who dressed in her brother's clothes and was caught in the rain. Without a word she settles down in a corner by herself. Only an occasional sniffle tells us she is still there.

Following the rain it becomes colder. About nine o'clock an awe-inspiring electrical storm breaks. The artillery of the heavens begins. Giant firecrackers split the air, their terrific concussions leaving us momentarily stunned. A nearby hit and the car rocks tipsily.

The little girl begins to pray; softly at first, like the purring of a cat. Then louder and louder until we can distinguish:

"Thy will be done as it is in Heaven. . . .
For Thine is the Power and the Glory."

# XI

O N the road the boys are developing their own point
of view. They have not yet acquired the definite
hobo outlook on life, but already they have lost many
of the old notions and they are losing more. They
see as through a glass darkly, but in the gloom they are
beginning to discern outlines of reality and bits of fact
upon which to anchor their judgments. Unlike boys
of their age at home, they hear and participate in discussions in box cars, not of the football prospects of
Notre Dame, or Carnera's boxing ability, or the World
Series, but of unemployment, government policies, machines, Communism, the workers' revolution, and religion. At home in high school or college, they might
with prompting discuss similar subjects, but the discussion would be abstract, impersonal. Failure would
result in loss of scholastic credit. On the road, the
discussion is concrete and personal, and failure may
result in loss of life. For, as the boys realize, upon
their ability to understand and to decide difficult, ob-
tuse questions or to leave these questions to leaders
capable of understanding and solving them depends their
future.

"It's the duty of the President," Texas said to me one day in September as an accommodation freight pulled through a land of plenty, "to see that nobody starves."

"Look at this," cut in a strange, blue-eyed lad, who had boarded the train furtively at the last stop, and waved a hand to include the abundant crops growing in the fertile valley. "Food! Food! Food! Crops! Everywhere! And me and you hungry. There's enough rotting on the ground to feed a million people and there's two million starving. It ain't right."

"A government that can't feed its own people," declared Whistler Will, spitting venomously at a signal post as we passed, "ain't a government at all."

The next day as we hit the cinders from a town which met us with a reception committee and clubs, Whistler Will said to me, "The government isn't half trying."

"The government," added someone, "does not intend to try."

Why doesn't the government intend to try? Every child tramp on the road would say, because the politicians are all grafters. Dishonest men seeking to fill their pockets at the expense of the public, they care nothing for the country and its people.

"Every mother's son of them is crooked."

"Show me a politician and I'll show you a crook."

"Listen, they got more honest men behind the bars than they have on the bench."

Once in a while, however, you find a boy who doesn't blame officeholders.

"Politicians can't do anything.   It's the bankers that hold the strings," said Boo Peep one day as we talked of this and that.

Wise and mature are many other ideas of boy tramps. One afternoon, on top of a box car rolling over the prairie, the boys began talking, as transients are forever talking, of prospects of work.

"Maybe things will pick up, now that booze is back," said one lad.

"Booze, hell," contradicted Slim Jim.   "It's bread, not beer, the country needs."

"And we can't get that," Bill finished belligerently, "until the worker gets stabilized wages and the farmer stabilized prices for his products.   See all those farmers back there by that mill.   If they could sell their grain for a fair price, they'd be buying stuff today from the cities and we'd have jobs."

"You capitalistic fools," sneered a Communist, "the only thing to do is to sweep out all the old crooks and old grafters and begin all over."

"You mean clean out one bunch," agreed Texas, "and put in another bunch."

"Sure," supported Happy Joe, "it's just one bunch of crooks or another bunch.   All are after the cash."

Every group of boy tramps contains a Communist. Bolshevism is spreading rapidly.   In the future it will spread more rapidly when it loses its foreign association, its newness, and acquires, as it inevitably will, a reputation for daring and a tradition for service. Practically the only group which will speak for the homeless man and the young tramp is the Communist. And the lads on the road are becoming converts.

The older transients, it is true, resist Communism. They have a mental hold-over of war psychology, the anti-Red drives of Palmer, and a belief in the American success story, which will not let them accept the new doctrines. For boys and girls, Communism offers school, hope and adventure.

"I'd rather be a Red than starving and dead," they say, and by the thousand.

Too young, too vital, to retreat from this world, they want some chance, some reward, while they are living.

To date Communism has spread slowly because of the character of the Communists. Too often they were personally offensive men who insulted instead of converting. Lately, Communism is being preached by some of the American-born and with more success.

"But you really ought to attend this meeting," Dressy said to me, as we sneaked out of evening prayer at a mission. "Five hundred of us are going to be there in the basement of the building and there isn't even one Jew speaker."

The boys, unlike the older transients, have no pronounced racial prejudice. They dislike the Communists not because they are Jews or Communists but be-

cause they are, as likely as not, disagreeable fellows—
"always arguing."

Of patriotism the boys appear to have not a shred.
They do not have any more feeling of loyalty to America
than they have to the South Pole. To them their country means nothing as an entity. Pride of race some still
have, but the race is a foreign one. Loyalty to a church
few still know, but the church is the Church of Rome.
Of service to the state, duty to the nation, the boys know
nothing and are willing to render less. That the government owes them a living all would agree. That they
owe the government anything none would admit. The
older men who served the country in the World War
might be willing to serve again. The younger ones
will serve only when forced.

"If they're going to shoot me, they can shoot me here.
I'll be God-damned if I go," said Sawbones, the ex-
medical student. "One of the things I hated about the
university was drill."

"If you don't go they'll put you in jail. If you do
go you'll be shot," said Slim Jim. "I'd rather go to
jail."

"Look at him," said Pete, pointing to an army officer
getting out of a government car, "all shined up, and who
pays for all that stuff?"

"They'll never wrap Old Glory around my blood-
stained body if I can help it," said Boris as we stood before a war memorial plaque in a small Wisconsin town.
"They can shoot me, but I won't go."

The most common and practically the only objection of the boy tramps to the Civilian Conservation Corps is that in the event of trouble the corps would have to fight. Lately, of course, deserters from the camps have added other objections. In March, 1933, all boys would have enlisted with enthusiasm—save for the objection to war service. Three months later the conservation camps were being called "prison"; five months later they were referred to as "army chain gangs"; ten months later as "Roosevelt roosts."

"I've been in jail twice, and three years in a reformatory," said a lanky youth dressed in the army khaki, which you learn to associate with deserters from the Civilian Conservation Corps, "and I've lived three months at Sally's in Chicago, but that army chain gang was worse than any."

And if the boys believe they owe little to the government they owe less to the social agencies. Missions are "places where you get sermons and sour stew." The Salvation Army, "Sally steals from the poor in this country to feed the rich in England." Municipal relief stations are "city rat holes." Community chests, Travelers' Aid, and welfare stations in general are called—always disparagingly—simply "they."

Stealing and begging, the only means by which the boys can obtain any material goods, are regarded, and sensibly, as occupations. Stealing, as the youths practice it, is always a form of sneak thievery. While they defend and admire the big crimes, bank holdups, kidnappings, mail robberies, they never seem to consider them as possibilities. The majority lack the nerve to "pull a big job." Few have courage enough to undertake even a first-class "prowl." An article snatched from an open counter, a purse yanked out of a woman's hand, a blanket or a coat taken out of a parked car, a coat jerked off a clothes line, pants hooked out of a window —these are the crimes that the child tramps commit.

They steal food and clothing because of need and because they know that, if they are caught, the penalty will be mild. A bakery truck driver catching a boy stealing buns will, most likely, let him go—and perhaps give him the buns. A housewife catching a boy stealing a bottle of milk will merely order him to drop it. Farmers may sic a dog on the boys in the garden, but more often they will give food if asked. "Stealing," in the child tramps' lexicon, does not exist. It is just "luck."

"Frank had some luck today" means Frank stole something and got by.

A few of the younger transients try to rationalize and justify theft. They see in the world not honest merit rewarded, but scorned, and dishonest cunning elevated and admired.

"Why is it," more than one boy tramp asked me, "if you steal a dollar's worth of shoelaces, they put you in jail for ten years, but if you steal a million dollars they make you a governor of a state?"

"Here's a guy who robs a bank with a machine gun," explained Jack reading a True Crime Story, "and the cops put him in jail for life.  Here's another guy who robbed ten banks and they make him governor."

"Yes, and he didn't have guts enough to fight with cops and guns either," vehemently agreed Nick.  "He robbed widows and orphans.  He stole from the poor and gave it to the rich.  One thing I like about a machine gun bandit, he's got guts.  Those other slimy skunks sneak in where everybody trusts them and then they lam with the dough."

"It ain't stealing," defended Tony as we prepared a meal from a chicken caught in a grove and a sack of potatoes lifted from a parked truck.  "It ain't stealing when you're hungry and willing to work and you can't get nothing to eat.  You don't take nothing away from anybody who needs it.  You just ask enough to live on.  That's all.  And you are willing to work; if you can't get work, why, you're entitled to help yourself."

Begging is so common that the boys and girls regard it entirely as commercial; no moral principle is involved.  They beg when they believe police will not catch them and they will be successful.  When the stem is too tough, they "do not hit it."

Toward sex, the boys and girls have an attitude of healthy young pagans.  Their lives are not the kind that permit very high moral standards.  Sex is a normal part of existence.  Continence depends upon absence of opportunity, not upon virtue.  Some boys were a little worried about masturbation and "wondered if a person would go crazy if he did it too much."  Others were afraid of disease.   No girls feared pregnancy: "If you're wise there's no danger."

Perverts among the older men attempt to influence the boy's attitude toward perversion, but without much success.   The boys have a healthy aversion to it.

Prostitution is regarded as a normal occupation by both boys and girls.   They say "She is a whore," just as others might say "She is a school-teacher."   The term is descriptive.   That is all.   Some girls pride themselves on the fact that they "either got cash or liked him." "What is the difference between getting paid and doing it for nothing?   I can't see any."

And yet marriage and babies are something different and almost sacred to many.

"Gee, I like kids," said Vera, as we watched some ragged urchins at play.   "I like kids better than anything else in the world."

"A girl is lucky to get a guy who can support her these days," said Dot.   "And when she does she ought to be good to him."

"Some day I'm going to have a home," said Meg, "and a good man and a couple of kids and an extra bed-room where Mother can stay.   She'll take care of the kids so I won't have to stay in all the time."

Others are scornful of marriage.

"No wedding bells for me, brother," said Red, a sandy-haired, tough little girl, as she listened for the bell of a freight engine.   "I don't want to wash any man's socks and have a bunch of dirty kids around the house. I want to be free to go where I like and when I like. Nobody's going to boss me."

Practically all boys and girls on the road, whether Communists or not, believe that America is going to have a revolution soon if things do not improve. They are vague as to who is going to lead it and how it is to be brought about, but almost all agree that trouble is imminent.

"We can't stand this forever."

"Hell is going to pop some day now."

"As soon as somebody gives the signal, there'll be plenty of hell breaking loose."

"No use bellyaching now, we gotta fight."

These and similar opinions are common in any group discussing the imminence of revolution.

On the day when the Florida assassin attempted to shoot President-elect Roosevelt, and shot Mayor Cermak of Chicago, I was with the boys in a jungle cave in the North. The news came as we were preparing for sleep. About nine P. M. Boo Peep came bursting in out of the darkness.

"They got Roosevelt," he cried. "Geez, they got somebody at last, and the mayor of Chicago, and maybe Hoover too."

Everybody asked questions. Jubilation was intense. Hoping that this was the signal which would touch off the revolution, we deserted our cave and went uptown to learn the truth.

About midnight we came trailing back into the cave, very dejected. The assassin had missed. The revolution had not started, and the night was bitterly cold.

Still, as we warmed ourselves, I felt a change in the boys. The ragamuffins of an hour or two ago were beaten, dispirited. These boys were dejected but in a fighting mood. One of the lowly and oppressed had dared the thunder. While he had missed, his action would not be forgotten.

"Maybe this will show some of those goddam bankers and high-ups something to wake them up," said Slim Jim. "I'd like to shoot the bastard that foreclosed Dad's home."

"But you'd miss, goddam you, you'd miss," Nick declared bitterly. "Why do they always have to miss? If I get a chance I won't miss."

Although there is agreement that a revolution is coming, child tramps feel no class solidarity. They have seen their elders at home and on the road make a mess of things too often to believe that the workers, alone, will effect a successful revolt.

"The workers could do it," Texas admitted to me at a soap-box meeting, "but they won't. They're too damn' dumb. You never saw a working stiff who wouldn't cut another working stiff's throat for a nickel."

"What we need is somebody to tell us what to do," said Boris early one winter morning as we witnessed a brutal police assault upon a dozen unoffending transients cowering in the frozen shade of a building. "We don't know what to do and so the bulls beat us and the Christians steal our soup and the judges send us to jail."

"But we'll learn," little Pete piped from the depths of an old camel-hair coat. "We'll learn. Oh, boy, how we'll learn. And then—"

"Learn, hell!" Nick contradicted. His face was still sore from a beating he had received two days previously at a city hall when, in company with a hundred others, he had protested the serving of rancid cheese and moldy bread at a mission. "Learn that the cops will only knock hell out of you, that's what you'll learn. Still," his melancholy face brightened momentarily, "I don't care. I sure kicked one cop in the nuts."

In spite of fights with police and battles with hunger and cold, the boys are optimistic as youth is ever optimistic. Away from home and living on their own, they are not a little proud of themselves.

"A fellow does not have to starve in America if he knows the ropes."

"Well, if the worst comes to the worst, I can always live at the missions."

"You just gotta use your head a little bit and you can always get by."

And yet they wonder how long this is going to last. They "don't want to be a bum!" They will "take anything if they can get it."

"Anything to get off the road," Texas said to me one

morning over coffee in a river camp during the second year of our friendship. "I've seen enough of the country. One city is just like another. And if a guy keeps traveling around too much, he becomes a bum. And I don't want to be a bum."

# XII

## PRESTIGE STANDARDS

EVERY group has certain standards formulated by its own laws and the exigencies of its physical life. All must conform to these standards. Every group has certain ideals created out of its hopes and dreams. All may aspire to these ideals. Childhood is the time for teaching the standards; youth the time for inculcating the ideals. We have seen what some of the standards of the young tramps are. Forced to steal or go hungry, to beg or go naked, to sacrifice their pride and to prostitute their bodies in order to live, they have dropped many of the standards of childhood. But what are the ideals of the boys and girls on the road? How do they differ from others at home?

They differ little so far as the first ideal is concerned. Home, high school, and childhood have paved the way for admiration of physical size and strength. The football player, the champion golfer, the acrobat, the dancer are admired by all persons at some time during youth and adolescence.

The admiration of high school youths for strength and agility differs from that of boys and girls on the bum. On the road the strong live and the weak die. Boys and girls lacking in unusual strength themselves

A couple of bindle stiffs enjoying a cigarette in the sun

Two boys on the bum enjoying the photographer's cigarettes. They did not know they were being snapped

Watching for the red lights of the yard

are proud to be votaries of the strong. Every gang of child tramps has one or two members with outstanding physical strength and ability. Often, as in labor unions, these larger boys are the leaders.

"A guy's got to have some size to get by," remarked Boo Peep to me one day as we saw a giant of a hobo walk insultingly by a small railroad detective and board a train as nonchalantly as lighting a cigarette while two dozen of us remained cowed by the officer's club and badge. "Now if I was bigger I wouldn't have to take nothing from nobody."

"Notice how tough he is to the little guys," he observed later pointing to a man behind a mission relief desk. "And how he smiles at muscle."

"Look," Pete pulled out his mission work ticket and shook it bitterly under my nose, "that's the fifth time in succession that they put me to work cleaning out the toilets and they give those big guys a soft job next to the grub in the kitchen."

"A small guy may be quick," philosophically commented Texas as we witnessed the termination of a long and bloody jungle fight between two older transients, "and look like a million dollars when the fight starts, but he can't stand the gaff with a bigger man. The big guy always wins. Muscle has it in a fight. The bigger they are the harder they fall, on you."

The good little man who fought so gamely and in the early stages so well, only to be defeated by a good big man, stirred in his rags on the grass. Blood flowed from his bruised nose and broken mouth. A scarlet bubble rose from his left ear turned up to the sun. He breathed a fast torturous rasp and his sides heaved convulsively. The good big man rocked drunkenly on his feet. He held a dirty hand to his closed left eye. Swollen lips trickled drops of blood, but there was no doubt about his victory.

Size helps in fights. And fights occur frequently in the young tramps' world. There is present in all their contacts an undercurrent of rebellion against life, a constant irritation produced by hunger. They are mad at life. For the slightest cause fights occur between the boys, between older men, between men and boys, transients and police. A real or fancied right of property has been infringed. The jungle law is invoked and renders its decision.

Racial prejudice scarcely exists. Never have I seen a fight between national, racial or even religious groups that did not have some other motivation. Swede and Italian, Protestant and Catholic, white and black are brothers on the road.

Religious fights occur and frequently, but they are between believers and non-believers. Strangely enough, the Christians are the aggressors. Out of over a dozen fights I can recall but one in which the Christian did not strike first. The Lord of Battles must favor his faithful followers; in only one contest was his defender vanquished. The atheist always got licked. Fights between blacks and whites occur frequently in the South, but they are based on economic rivalry.

Important as it is, fighting ability is not the only reason for the boys' admiration of physical size. The child tramps are close to the hand worker. The casual laborer desired physical strength because physical strength was his stock in trade. It was a commodity commanding a definite price in the "slave markets" where employment agencies are. Large size and strength plus the ability to handle himself meant and still means, for the casual, a job. Time after time the young tramps see a factory employment manager walk down a line of applicants and select the young, the healthy, and the strong.

Girls, too, need strength. They need strength to work, to stand the rigors of their life. A girl has to be substantially as strong as a boy. She may not engage in as many fights, but the fights she engages in are just as bitter and important. I have seen a girl tramp fight with a policeman so well and so long that, if another cop had not come to his assistance, he would never have been able to put the girl in the squad car. As it was, she bit his ear and scratched his face until he was bleeding.

"Show me a broad," said thin Vera to me one day as we watched a bevy of large prostitutes leaving a house for a trip uptown, "who can make a dollar on the street who hasn't hips."

Physical prowess means not only victory in jungle

fights or success in applying for a position; it means survival on the road. Without physical strength the child tramps could not live. They could not endure the long walks, the nights without sleep, the days without food, the exposure to the elements and the risks of traveling, if it were not for a good reserve of strength. Boys and girls walk twenty miles of a day, stand all night on the couplings between two box cars or lie on the roof exposed to a cold rain, eat one meal next day, walk five miles and, still wearing their wet clothing, sleep the next night in a box car and awake in the morning without even a head cold. The feats of endurance and strength that they perform normally as a part of their existence seem incredible. Why they do not freeze to death, die of a cold, catch pneumonia, tuberculosis, or some other disease is unexplainable. Perhaps many do. Only the survivors remain on the road.

Physical prowess means ability to travel, and prestige accrues to the child tramp as to the older transient, according to his ability to ride without a ticket. Child tramps, in fact, rank themselves according to their ability to travel and the means of locomotion they use. At the head of the list, so far above as to be scarcely identified with child tramps, are the few youths who use the highways but never hitch-hike. They secure rides chiefly by watching the ads in the large city papers, often by inserting one offering to drive somebody on a long tour. The boys are well dressed, well man-

nered, and well spoken. Their expenses are paid. Often
they get a generous tip. Certainly, a recommendation.
They have, for the most part, some resources. Frequently they come from good homes. Below them are
the boys who hitch-hike, and at the bottom are the
ninety per cent or more who ride the rails.

Each class has its own distinctions. The boys who
ride in motor cars have little respect for the train riders,
who, in their eyes, are bums.

"I've been on the road for two years now," a well-
dressed youth explained his racket, "and I'm still not
a bum. I've never had to sleep in a mission. I've
never had to eat in a jungle. And I've never hit the
stem. If you've got a front you can get by most places.
I've got a little racket. I sell souvenirs at football
games, World Series, American Legion conventions,
state fairs, and any place. I've been to every big event
in the country in the last two years. I left home without a dime and today I got more than a dollar."

The ones riding trains have both respect and contempt for youths on the highways—respect because
the other boys have a good front, contempt because in
spite of the front they are broke.

"Look at him," a vile-smelling little urchin of fourteen pointed contemptuously to a clean boy of his own
age in a relief station. "He's a chump. Too good for
us, I suppose, he thinks he is. And yet he ain't got a
dime in his pocket, while I got forty-five cents; be-

sides, I spent over twenty cents getting drunk night before last."

And within the class of train riders, there are subclasses and distinctions even as there are among adult transients.

At the top of the hierarchy are the aristocratic "passenger stiffs" who ride nothing but through trains. These youths have a mania for speed. They have no purpose in life, so far as I could discover, beyond going from one place to another in the least possible time. In order to ride the fast trains they endure hunger, cold, privations. Generally they ride the blinds. When they cannot make the blinds they ride a step or the roof. Wherever there is a hand or foot hold they ride. On the whole, they are morose and uncongenial, easily provoked, and always offended. Life to them is to be lived with contempt, death to be greeted with scorn. They do not like missions. They do not like other young tramps. They do not like trainmen. They do not like each other. When compelled to associate with other boys and girls in jungles and in missions, they do so ungraciously, and only when forced. Passenger stiffs are almost always boys. I knew but one girl who regularly rode the blinds, and she rode to be with the boy she wanted. Passenger stiffs have no respect for 'boes who ride freights.

"Now if you want to pal with me," Jim's blue eyes looked challengingly into mine, "you got to be able to go places in a hurry. I had a pal once, but I quit when he lost his guts and took to freights. Me, I got kicked out of the station in Cleveland eleven times one night but next morning when the Century pulled into New York I was right up there on the tender."

Beneath passenger stiffs are the road bums who ride freights. They constitute about eighty-five per cent of all youthful vagrants. Yet even this group has its nobility and its proletariat. Boys and girls riding the California Fruit Express are but a step below passenger stiffs. Next come those who ride silk trains, and below them the red ball or manifest freight riders and, near the bottom, accommodation freights, and finally gondolas and granite cars.

Next to ability to travel and physical prowess in granting a child tramp prestige is ability—nerve might be a better word—to get by. As American life rewards the nervy sales promoter who forces his way into a house and his product upon a nation, so transient life rewards the boy or girl with plenty of brass.

"What I like about Nick," Buster is boasting of the virtues of his traveling companion, "is that he has plenty of guts. He can talk a guy at a mission into giving him a bed when everybody else is sleeping on the floor. We goes into Sally's in Chicago, and the first job he gets is in the kitchen. Before night he has enough food tucked away to carry us damn' near to Colorado. I seen him hit a man for a dime and get it right behind a cop's back. And when he did get pinched

one time in Kansas City, he talked so much that he
had the police sergeant and all the city dicks bawling.
They let him go and gave him half a buck. Yes, sir,
Nick sure has the guts."

\* \* \*

"The cop was watching us for over two blocks,"
Boris told of an adventure. "He saw Slim hit the
woman for a dime. I stood in the way. But he saw
her shell out. So when he catches us, and was going to
say something, you know what Slim did?"

"No."

"He throws a fit. Just like that, he falls over, his
mouth foaming and all twisted, his eyes rolling way
back, so we couldn't see anything but the white. He
grabbed his gut as if he was poisoned and groaned. The
cop and I pulled him over to the side of a building.
When I lifted him he felt all stiff-like. I put my coat
under his head. A man comes running out of a store
with a glass of water. Then Slim pretended he passed
out for a minute. He shook his head, came to, drank
the water and says, 'I'm all right now.' In a little
while he gets up and says, 'I'm sorry to have incon-
venienced you, gentlemen, but I had one of my spells.
Thanks for the assistance.' Just like that, using big
words and taking off his cap. We walks away and the
cop only says, 'Sure you can get on all right, boys?'
And we says, 'Sure.'"

Ability to talk is in itself a standard of prestige.

"Did you see me bullying the guy?" Happy Joe asked me as he seated himself next to me at a mission. A moment before he had been talking dramatically to an older transient a bench away. "I was trying out something. And, by God, it seems swell. He was be-lieving me, too, when I told it to him. I'm going to try it on the stem tomorrow and see how it works."

Lying is useful, because it assures success in begging. Success in begging means money, and the prestige that goes with money anywhere in America. In other circles the term "beggar" may carry odium, but among child tramps a good panhandler can always use a dime. A dime buys tobacco, liquor, food, clothing. It cements friends and softens enemies. Ability to hit the stem—beg—successfully creates prestige for boy or man. Younger transients admire and follow him. Older ones admit him as an equal. Wherever he goes the clever child tramp can beg enough to live on.

Stem hitters are ranked in three classes according to what they panhandle and where. Boys and girls who hit the stem for food rank lowest; boys and girls who hit the back porches are next; boys and girls who hit the stem for money are higher, and the highest of all are the ones who hit the houses for cash. The latter occupation takes not only nerve, but brains and per-sonality. The boy or girl successful at it has money and praise.

Praise and money go also to the boy or girl successful at stealing, and scorn and derision to the ones who fail.

"That guy's dumb." Happy pointed disgustedly at Fred. "He don't know nothing. I sets him before a stand, and I gets the guy talking about something else and even his back turned, and do you think he would heist a couple of oranges? No, he just stands there dumb-like, until it is too late."

\* \*

We stood on a hill in early September overlooking Lake Culver. Below us and to the right spread one of the finest military schools in the nation. Rich boys were playing touch ball on the athletic field. Texas, Boo Peep and I watch them.

"I'd like to be back in school," remarks Texas.

"I wouldn't mind it," agrees Boo Peep, "but not in that school. Rich kids are always dumb."

"How do you know?" I ask.

"Well, I know because my brother used to work on the estates at Lake Forest, and he told me that if any of the rich kids lost a key, they didn't know how to make a wire open a lock, or spring it or anything. They were dumb."

"Something pretty interesting happened to me in Chi the last time I was there," Dressy bragged as he brushed his coat carefully. "I think I made a connection."

I waited for him to go on.

"You know it was all kind of an accident, too. I was just legging down a street when a car pulled up to the curb, and a couple of guys got out. And the guy who was driving the car was Jimmy Genario. I recognized him just like that, and I says, 'Hello, Jimmy.' And he says 'Hello' and goes into the building.

"Well, I didn't have very much to do so I sticks around thinking maybe he might come out in a little while. I felt kind of tired. The sun was shining hot. I sits down on the running board of the coupe to rest, and just sort of thinks 'Here I'm sitting on Jimmy Genario's car' when some cops come up in a Ford squad car. And one gets out and he makes out a tag because Jimmy's car is parked right next to a fire hydrant, but hell, I never noticed it before.

"I see the cop is going to put a tag on the car, and I say to him 'Here, you can't do that.'

" 'Like hell, I can't,' says he, putting the tag on the wheel.

" 'No,' I say. 'Don't you know who's car that is?'

"And he says, 'No, and I don't give a damn.'

"And I says, "Well, that's Jimmy Genario's car.'

"And he says, 'Is that Jimmy Genario's car?'

"And I says, 'Yes, that's Jimmy Genario's car.'

"And he says 'Hell, I never knew that was Jimmy Genario's car.' And he tears up the ticket and gets in his Ford and drives away.

"So, I think, it was lucky I was there or else Jimmy

might have got a ticket. I didn't have very much to do, and I waits around for a couple of hours. After a while Jimmy Genario comes hustling out. He is going to drive off, and I tells him. I tell him about the cop. And he says to me—you know what he says to me?—he says 'Thanks.'"

# XIII

ABOUT what do boys and girls on the road talk? Brokers discuss the stock market. Baseball fans talk about the pennant race. Greenwich Villagers argue over art and philosophy. Communists predict the day when the Red Army will march. Mothers talk of babies, girls of dates; business men about business; musicians of music. And the child tramps—they talk of what?

\* \* \*

Travel, mostly, and food and clothing, and adventures on the road and begging and stealing, and of sex too. Over three hundred samples of conversation were collected under all conditions and at all times. They were collected in the morning before breakfast and at evening around a jungle camp-fire. They were collected on the tops of box cars and in waiting rooms of missions. They were collected while tramping in the rain and while lolling in the sun. And the main worry and concern of both boys and girls is traveling.

"It doesn't make no difference what train you take;

just so long as it's on the S. F. and southbound, you'll get there."

"You ride two nights and the second morning you throw away your overcoat."

"Watch for the red lights, and then jump and run before the bulls will get you."

"And when you get in the yards, see, watch for the second signal tower and then a switchman's shanty. Drop off there and you can't miss it."

"Take a Rock Island going South to the junction."

"On the way East we run into some hard luck in St. Louis."

\* \*
\*

Next to travel, the road kids talk most of clothes. Clothes, vitally important, are extremely difficult to obtain. A pair of shoes wears out in a week. Even the toughest overalls need repairs in a fortnight. Second-hand coats cannot stand the strain of being worn twenty-four hours a day in all weathers. They break not in one place but in a dozen, suddenly disintegrating into nothing. In almost every jungle some boys will be inspecting, some girls repairing, clothing.

"But your shoes—hell, you wear out a pair of shoes and then where are you."

"A jacket is oke until it gets cold. Then I want something around my legs."

"I don't like a pair of shoes too big, because I kick the toe out the first week."

"A sweater is all right if you got something over it, or a newspaper under it. If not the wind goes through—"

"Listen, the first thing to do is tighten the buttons. When you get an old coat or pair of pants, go over it, see, and tighten the buttons, and sew up the linings and any place that is loose and it will last twice as long."

"Grease 'em. Hell, you always want to grease a pair of shoes. They'll last longer then."

"Thirty-five cents is a lot of money to pay for a pair of pants."

"Always turn your cap inside out when you're riding open."

"A skirt helps a girl on the main stem but it's a lousy thing to wear in a box car."

"Three safety pins, and you wouldn't know I had tore it."

\* \* \*

Clothing and travel are important in the lives of the young tramps. So are cops. The boys and girls learn to fear, to respect, and, strangely enough, at times to like them. While many of the older transients hate all officers, having apparently a complex against them, the young ones have no such attitude. Policemen have chased them, may have struck them, put them in jail; but policemen have also befriended them, fed them, given them clothes, rescued them from storm and cold. Almost all officers have children of their own; others remember days of poverty, childhoods of want. They understand and sympathize with the youthful vagrants. The boys and girls in their turn understand and sympathize with the cops.

"You don't have to ever be afraid of a fat cop, unless he is drunk. He'll always give you the breaks."

"I just go right up to a cop and ask him."

"Santa Fé bulls are tough, boy, are they tough."

"And the cop says to me, 'Keep right on traveling, sister,' and I did."

"When you see a small cop, who isn't shaved, look out; he's tough."

"I just heists it off the Wop's stand and tucks it under my coat, when a cop comes around the corner."

"A great big cop takes me into a restaurant and says, 'Here, Bill, give this girl all she wants to eat and no funny business, understand.'"

Police officers interfere with the young tramps' chief means of livelihood—begging. The boys can live after a fashion at missions; the girls by their own initiative or the resources in jungles. Both choose, in the majority of cases, to live independently. Occasionally they work to earn clothing and food, but ordinarily they must rely upon begging. They consider ways and means of begging, techniques and prospects, towns and parts of towns in the same way that a group of traveling salesmen or house-to-house canvassers consider their trade. People do not want to buy insurance or to give alms to beggars. It is the task of the salesman or young beggar to overcome this "resistance." Rapidly, indeed, are the boys and girls learning tricks of trade and exchanging experiences.

"Fast and hard I hits the stem right after the rain and I makes forty-five cents in less than an hour."

"I stays pretty near all afternoon in that block but I finally gets a dime from a red-headed girl in front of a restaurant."

"When a gray old lady comes to the door, act kinda scared."

"A Jew won't give nothing. He likes to turn you down."

"A young married woman is good that way, she'll pretty near always give you an old shirt of her husband's."

"Straight sob, I always plays it.  Tell 'em you're hungry and want something to eat."

"When I hit the stem, I like to be clean; then nobody suspects till you ask them."

"I never worked the houses around a Catholic Church that I didn't get something."

* *

The child tramps beg in order to eat.  They must eat in order to live.  Fully half their daily hours and more of their energy is expended in a quest for food.  With the healthy, robust appetites of youths living an active life, they are eternally hungry.  Food is the motive of almost all their actions.  They travel in order to eat.  They work, they beg, they steal, and they give their bodies in order to eat.  Food is an everlasting subject of conversation among child tramps, who talk of techniques for acquiring and of methods of improving food.

"Almost any bakery will give you day-old bread and maybe buns and stuff if you hit the night foreman about ten o'clock."

"I always put lots of pepper in the mission stew.  It gives it zip."

"Throw your card on the table and then pick it up as though he punched it, see, and maybe you can save a meal."

"If I have a ring of bologna, a loaf of rye bread with caraway seeds in it, and a piece of cheese I don't have to get off a freight for two days."

"You can pretty near always get a piece of sausage from a German butcher."

"When you cook a chicken be sure and take all the guts out. Then you won't get that sour taste on the breast."

"An onion makes almost anything taste better."

"And the doughnuts were fresh. You didn't have to dunk 'em."

*       *
*

Next to food, the girls as well as the boys talk most frequently of fights and quarrels. In the lives of the boy tramps contests are common. In the lives of the girls these fights are stirring dramatic incidents relieving monotony and giving drama and zest to living. That the fight may be over a girl and that the victor may claim his age-old reward adds to the excitement. So does participation of the girls themselves in the fights. These fights are not the sham contests of the playgrounds, but earnest blood-and-flesh fights of man and man, boy and boy, or boy and man, girl and man, girl and girl. Sometimes the fight is with a railroad official, a townsman, or a cop. Always the fight is long and bloody and its cause almost anything.

"The big coward. He started running even before the little guy swings at him."

"No, I wouldn't start a fight, but I wouldn't mind if the other guy started it."

"He wasn't so tough after Red got through with him."

"Then wham! he gets one on the kisser."

"Just like that he draws a knife and slashes at the big guy's belly."

"When he swings he swings from the floor."

"All of a sudden he jumps up and runs, and the fat guy after him socking away at the back of his neck."

"He was a dirty fighter. He bit and kicked."

"And he hits him with a blackjack so hard that all the shot falls out."

\*  
\*  \*

Fights are part of the adventures of a child tramp's life but not all. The boys and girls live dangerously. Never is there an uneventful day in their lives. Dramatic incidents are not rare. Stark tragedy and ironic comedy are not unknown. Around camp-fires and after meals the group exchanges adventures and discusses deeds on the road.

"I just grabbed the step in time. The train pulled me and dragged the soles off my shoes."

"The guy asks me to his room, and I says, 'Go to hell, you goddam wolf.' "

"Fred slipped and bumped me, and I thought both of us were going over the side."

"A traveling salesman took me clear to Montana but in Billings a sheriff asks are we married."

"And there waiting for me to come out of the cornfield was farmer Silo, himself."

"Two girls were traveling with us then."

"I was sneaking down the tracks when a switchman says to me, 'Come on in here, girlie, and warm yourself,' and I goes in, and four guys try to make me."

"The girl smiles at me and says, 'Sure, kid, come on in.' "

"And I says, 'I was just leaving town,' and the cop says, 'See that you do, sister, see that you do.' "

"The state cop turns me back, but the next day I steals some California license plates off a big car in Las Vegas, and we sails right over the line."

Although the young tramps try to live independent of bread lines and welfare stations, they must rely upon them in times of need. Every boy and many girls have lived at one in the past. Every one will live at one again in the future.    Relief agencies and policies are discussed frequently.

"You gotta work for your breakfast there."

"You just sign your name, and the man hands you out a ticket."

"I always hits one just at supper time.    Then I don't have to work."

"And they let you lie down any time during the day."

"And she asks me was I going to have a baby, and I says 'no.' "

"Bossing you around like you was a bunch of cattle."

"Swill, that's all you get at that place, swill."

"When you go into any new mission, look kinda scared."

* *
*

To look at the average young tramp, you would think that he or she is little concerned with personal appearance.    Yet the condition of road rags worries either boy or girl just as much as high school clothing styles worry more fortunate youngsters.    A boy is self-conscious about a dirty face, long hair, a fuzz-covered chin; a girl will be ashamed to appear on the streets in too poor clothing.    Proud of a new pair of shoes or a new cap, a boy will strut, a girl will preen and bridle.    If he is old enough to shave, the boy likes to carry a razor. The girl almost always carries a toothbrush and a powder puff.

"A guy always feels better after a haircut."

"I always comb my hair before breakfast, no matter where I am."

"Geez, when I got the new outfit from the lady, nobody would take me for a bum."

"It pays to brush your teeth, even with a poor toothbrush."

"I always wear some kind of a brassière. It makes me feel better."

"I save my necktie and always wear it on Sundays."

"You don't have to worry too much about your clothes, just so you keep them clean."

"You always want to carry a couple of safety pins with you."

"A good cap, Shorty, and a necktie sets you off better than anything else."

\* \* \*

Another common subject of conversation is boys and girls.

"Geez, I had a swell boy friend in Alabama."

"Sam has a girl in New Jersey."

"Picture your guy back in Georgia. Hell, that's Clark Gable."

"Any girl likes it, but some pretend they don't want to be kissed."

"He smiles at me all the while I was eating, and when I was leaving he says 'Want a lift, girlie?' "

"And when I was leaving she says, 'Take me with you.' "

"There's a girl coming with them from Chi."

"Lots of girls can flip a train as good as any man."

Almost as common a conversational subject as boys or girls is liquor.

"Frank was drunk and the dope starts arguing with the cop."

"If you want to get drunk, go ahead, I'll watch you."

"And was I sick next morning."

"Not just dehorn but good whiskey."

"If you eat a dozen raw tomatoes, next day you feel fine."

Other subjects about which the young tramps talk are tobacco, war, sexual perversion, murders, crimes, work, mechanical devices, and home.

"Three long butts I kipped right in front of the entrance."

"And the social worker asks, 'How do you keep from having babies?' And I just laugh."

"But the French Foreign Legion can lick any other outfit in the world. Baby, that outfit is tough."

"If the Japs start a war, I wonder if Russia will get in."

"He was another of those guys who want to use a kid for a woman."

"—and he cut her body up and put it in a basket."

"Four men enter the bank with machine guns. They started firing as they came out."

In a study of the conversations of the young tramps one sees much of their life and point of view. Food, clothing, and traveling play the important part in their conversations that they play in their lives. Begging, policemen, fights, relief policies all belong to the child tramps' existence. Their concern with clothing and appearances, with girls and boys, with liquor, reveal the normal adolescents' attitudes and curiosity. It is not at all strange that they should discuss these subjects.

It is strange, however, to find boys and girls of sixteen to eighteen practically never talking about school or sports. The young tramps evidently have had little opportunity for either.

A comparison of the conversational subjects of the young tramps with those of older transients reveals important differences. In another study of mine, over four hundred conversations of transients and homeless men were recorded and analyzed. Comparing the two studies, we find that the older men talk most about food, clothing, relief policies, liquor, work, traveling, fights, and homosexuality.

Both groups discuss nearly the same subjects, although in a different order of importance. In the older men's conversation, food and clothing come first and women not at all. Traveling to them is not the adventure, nor is it perhaps the necessity, that it is to the child tramps. Older homeless men frequently are residents of a city. They discuss homosexuality much more frequently and in a different light; while the boys speak disapprovingly of it, the older men discuss homosexuality frankly as a common and pleasant practice.

In addition to differences in subject matter, there is a difference in expression and presentation of subject between the two groups. The older men, except when they are angry, usually talk with moody, expressionless face and voice. Their auditors listen with sneering or contemptuous inattention. They rarely smile, and they never laugh. Seldom do they tell an anecdote for the sake of the anecdote. Life to them is a bitter cup with only the dregs left. The child tramps are more joyful. They tell a story with expression and gestures. They listen to one with interest and amusement. Not only do they laugh, but they interject humorous comments on the story, and one tale leads to another as naturally as it does in a convention of traveling salesmen. It is quite likely that another study made of conversations of older homeless women and younger girl tramps would reveal similar age differences.

The young tramps talk of many things, but never, in groups, of home. To talk of home might arouse old thoughts and happy memories, and tears might sneak into eyes grown hard and a little tired on the road.

# XIV

## TWO DIARIES

THE boy or girl tramps are ill equipped for keeping any literary record. Many carry a stub of pencil and a notebook, but these are practical necessities for writing directions and names of men, women, or firms who might give shelter or work. Some boys systematize note-taking, making records as carefully as business men keep track of daily sales. These records note the boy's success or failure in different towns and cities through which he has passed. Details are minimized, facts emphasized such as "fat woman in a big white house gave me three pork sausages, four cups of coffee and all the pancakes I wanted for breakfast. . . . A bull socked me as I was leaving the yards. Hostile town. . . . No use standing up for Jesus at —— mission. Nothing but beans and misery."

Still in the process of being recorded, the diaries are consulted and extended daily.

Blink meets Red in Toledo. He is on his way to Seattle. Red has just escaped from a state camp in California.

"Stay away from Dubuque," warns Red; "hostile town. But if you are near Sioux City, go there. Police

202

station meal cards. No questions asked. Just go to the window and he shoves out a card."

"Sioux City, you say?" inquires Blink, his one eye betraying interest. "Seems to me that's the place Frog Legs told me not to go to. You sure?"

"Just a second," Red's freckled face screws up worriedly. "I ain't sure." He reaches into a pocket in his third layer of shirts. "I'll give a look and see."

Out comes a small notebook, dirty and thumb-marked. Red scowls as he searches for the place, having the same trouble with his files that many business men have. He finds it. His face lights up and he smiles. The smile turns to incomprehension and disbelief. "No, I guess I was wrong. It ain't Sioux City I was thinking about. It must have been some place else."

The boys discuss relief policies, police vigilance, and the possibilities of panhandling in different towns and cities, referring from time to time to notebooks, warning each other away from some towns, recommending others.

Under the pretext that I was going to follow the same route, I copied entries from two.

The first diary is Blink's, the one-eyed Dutch boy from Pennsylvania. He had been on the road a year when I met him. He had two good eyes when he left his father's farm. Now he has but one. A bloody socket forms a small and ever-weeping cave on the left side of his face. Tears streak his cheek, furrowing the dirt and coal soot, leaving a strange moist scar alongside

his nose.  He lost his eye when a live cinder blew into
it on the Santa Fé.  All night he suffered while companions probed for the cinder with dirty-handkerchief
covered sticks.  In the morning a special agent took him
to a physician, but the eye was already gone.

From his diary I copied the first month's entries of
the days when he had two glims and the world, he believed, was an oyster.

Aug. 24, 1932.  Fight with the old man.  He can't boss me.
Packed clothes and left.  Got a ride on truck full of furniture
going to Louisville.  Two men driving.  Good guys, bought
me my meals.  Slept in truck.  Men took turns driving.  We
stole some melons and apples from a farmer.

Aug. 27.  Truck burned out bearing near Covington.  Picked
ride to Cinci.  Man gave me a quarter and bought me a good
meal.  Paid 10c for bed and 15c for breakfast.  Met Frank.
Took me to soup kitchen.  Two meals for three hours work
washing walls.

Aug. 30.  Chicago.  Picked ride with salesman.  Let me drive
car.  Bought meals.  Four days in Chicago.  Good town.
Everything free.  Met Al.  Showed me how to get seven free
meals a day.

Sept. 1.  Me and Al got caught raiding fruit store.  Cop let
us go if we'd scram.  Separated from Al.  Grant Park.  Lots
of big houses.  Plenty to eat.  Every house wanted to feed me.
Got 14c cash and made 80c cutting grass and cleaning basement.
Old lady gave me a pair of shoes and sweater.  Good town but
small.

Sept. 2.  Momence.  Slept in farmer's barn last night.  Helped
with chores for breakfast.  Swell apple jelly.  Man wanted me
to stay and work all winter.  No money.  Nothing doing I tells

him, but I helps out with chores just the same. Lady makes me a pick lunch. Hit a man in front of hotel for dime. Caught by cop. Two hours to get out of town.

Sept. 6. St. Anne. Lots of Catholics, but all tight. Plenty of handouts but you have to eat outside on porch. No money. Dog bit me. Little fuzzy white dog as I was talking to big fat lady. Went to convent and hit sisters for pair of pants. Told them my mother was sick. Got pants from priest and 10c. Slept in corn crib.

Sept. 7. Walked Papineau, hitting farmers on way. Plenty to eat. Swell chicken at one house and all I want. Offered job. Help farmer shingle barn. Ask him for 50c. Offer only 25c. Nothing to it. Didn't like him anyway. Made 10c helping truck driver shift load. Going wrong way or I'd rode with him. Papineau small burg. N. G.

Sept. 8. Woodland. Tough town. Marshal boots me soon as I hits the main drag. Picked ride with farmer to Goodwine. Wanted me to dig potatoes. 35c a day. Look place over. Have to sleep with cows and maybe don't get any money, too. Nothing in it. Met Slim. Says no good down the line. We killed four chickens and made stew. I got a loaf of bread from a girl.

Sept. 9. Walked part way from Cessna. Took freight Hooperton. Good town. Picked 40c from doorsteps and swell meals. Stayed down in jungles near river with four other guys for four days. Nothing to do and all we want to eat from farmer's field. Chicken every day and roast corn and potatoes. We even had can ice cream, from church picnic.

Sept. 10. Slept in paper box. Bummed swell breakfast three eggs and four pieces meat. Hit guy in big car in front of garage. A cop told me to scram. Rode freight Roessville. Small burg, but got dinner. Walked Bronson. N. G. Couple a houses. Rode to Sidell. N. G. Hit homes for meals and turned down. Had to buy supper 20c. Raining.

Sept. 11. Villa Grove. Rode with truck. Good town. Raining when I hit first house. Woman gave me three eggs, two big pieces of meat. Cream and corn flakes, cookies, jell and all the coffee I want. Ask lots of questions. Man in house, too. He gives me a dime when I go. Made thirty cents hitting stem. A junction. Took train. Friendly. Good for supper and that's all.

Sept. 12. Shelbyville. Cop picked me up. Sent to jail, had to work two hours for dinner and supper. Stayed in jail all night. Six guys of us. N. G. Got out before breakfast. Walked with Shorty to Baxter. Small burg. N. G. Rode with farmer to Clarksburg. N. G. Got handout from farm girl, bacon and bread. Me and Shorty came back to ask for drink of water and she says, "Sic 'em," to big gray dog. Dog jumped at Shorty, but Shorty socks it. I gets a club. Dog chases us a mile until we get to gravel and a lot of bricks. Boy did we give it to him then.

Sept. 15. Slept out with Shorty and girl for three nights. Two in farmer's barn, one in parked truck. We got all we want to eat from farmers for helping the work. Shorty got a pair of overalls. Went to Mode. N. G. Small.

Sept. 16. St. Elmo. Good. 20c and a new pair of socks. Shoemaker fixed shoe for nothing.

Sept. 20. Granite City. Swell guy give me a ride from St. Elmo. Bought lunch. Good town. Made 80c helping guy build fence. Spent 5c for ice cream cone. 10c movie. Swell show. All about gangsters and true to life. Swell girl in picture. Slept under loading platform. Rain. Got wet. Hit woman for breakfast and dry shirt. Got sweater.

Sept. 22. Cop caught me with pockets full of apples. One hour to scram. Took freight. Going East St. Louis.

The second diary is Simple Sam's. He is a cross-eyed Jewish boy from New York, and had been almost three years on the road when I met him. For some reason he did not like Jews, hated rabbis, and delighted to live among Gentiles.

Although still very young, Sam had already acquired the outlook of the chronic tramp. He was called Simple Sam because of his egotistic habit of saying that everything was simple. "How do you go from Atlanta to New Orleans without going through Mississippi? That's simple"—and he would give directions, invariably wrong. "You want to get a pair of shoes on the stem? That's simple"—and he would give the most complicated and difficult directions.

The excerpts from his diary are for the spring of 1933.

April 6. Marshalltown, Iowa. Pop. 20,000. Good. Made 85c hitting back doors and all I want to eat. Pd 15c for knife. Best place near big school. Simple.

April 7. Hit five small towns today. Albion population 400, Union. Gifford and Abbot, population about 100-200. Picked up thirty cents, four meals and a pair of shoes. Easy to get rides. Lots of farmers wanted me to work. Simple.

April 8. Slept Hampton back of station. Good place old shed. Five others. Hit stem for breakfast. Got hitch to Livermore. Pop. 1000. Tough bull. Hit guy for dime in front of barber shop. Bull in shop. Comes out. Ride truck to Arnold. Small. Hit school teacher in small school. She all alone after school. Gives 25c and ride to Humboldt.

Humboldt N. G.   Three women sic dogs.   Take truck to
Fort Dodge.

April 9.   Fort Dodge.   Stem too tough.   Nobody gives guy
break.   Work for meals.   So bought breakfast 10c.   Picked
up five lunches, street crew shack, milk 7c. and ate lots pies
and cookies.   Ride to Algona in truck.   Gave driver part of
lunches.   He bought coffee.   Simple.

April 11.   Algona, pop. 4,000.   Good town.   Got dime and
meals.   Slept in farmer's barn.

April 12.   Estherville, pop. 4,000.   N. G.   Had to buy
lunch 5c.   Met bo.   Hit country for chicken.   Two ducks and
asks a girl at farm for loaf of bread.   She gives me a big hunk
and some cookies.   Met a frill on loose.   Says she is in love
with somebody else and nothing doing unless you got the dough
15c.   Nothing doing with me.

April 14.   Ride to St. James, Minnesota, pop. 3,000.   Good
town.   By big Catholic church made 20c and 30c for cleaning
yard and spading garden.   Woman give me old pair of shoes
and sweater.   Simple.

April 15.   Mankato.   Swell town.   Hit main drag 30c in
half hour.   Got quarter from lady in big parked car right down
town.   Lady gave me nine pancakes, four eggs and five cups
of coffee and two pieces of pie.   Simple.

April 16.   Sleepy Eye.   N. G.   Little preacher gives me a
dime.   Garage man tells me I best scram.   Go to New Ulm
after.   Bigger.   Good town.   Storekeeper gives me cheese and
crackers and milk.   Get 10c for washing windows in barber
shop and hair cut free.   Simple.

April 17.   New Ulm.   Farmers want you to work.   All I
want to eat.   Met Sue and Bob again.   Coming from Mpls.
We stay together two nights in lumber shed.   Hit stem for
meals cinch.'   Made 48c helping man put cement floor in ga-

rage.  Sue getting fat.  Bob says she isn't going to have kid.
They go to St. Louis, now.

Went with them to Albert Lea.  Good town.  Slept in basement old store.  Hit stem for 15c and breakfast.  Woman near
school gave me whole new suit when I help her trim bushes
and fix flower bed for day.  Also 10c.  Simple.

April 20.  Hit small towns, Manchester, Hartland, New
Richland.  All little burgs.  Got a new cap. pr. shoes, underwear in New Richland.  10c in Manchester.  Swell chicken
dinner in Hartland.  Slept in farmer's barns.  One night bull
got loose and pretty near wreck place before I get out.

April 25.  Montgomery pop. 1200.  N. G.  Women too
tough.  New Prague pop. 1600.  Fair.  Good eats but no
cash.

April 26.  Jordan.  Pop. 1000.  Got breakfast 5c.  Chaska.
Good.  Man wanted to buy me 50c dinner.  I say "Mister,
give me the 50c instead.  That will last me for a week."  Got
50c.  Pd. 10c patch shoe.  Woman gave me a good handout.
Half a cake.  Simple.

April 27.  Shakopee.  N. G.  Tough cop.  Can't hit the
stem.  Pick up truck to Mpls.  Good town.  Stem kinda tough.

And here the diary ended.

# XV

IMPORTANT as are the different elements and activities in their life, it is only when we see them united that we realize the child tramps are developing a tribal life of their own. Driven out of homes, unable to find work or to live in normal ways, they are developing, in the face of necessity, their own means of sustaining life and their own social habits, justifying their actions through their own folkways and system of morals. Within a year I saw Texas change not only physically but mentally. His frozen ears and stiff fingers were outward symbols of an inner change. From a bright, witty, American schoolboy, full of dreams and vigor, he had turned into a predacious, cunning person, whose habits and actions differed as much from those of the American schoolboy he had been as the habits and actions of a member of one African tribe differ from those of another. He had, in fact, dropped out of one tribe or nation and gone into another where the tribal life is different.

The first thing to notice about the tribal life of the boys and girls is the numerical size of the unit. The young tramps divide into gangs of a dozen or less. Larger units are cumbersome. Smaller units are not strong enough for protection. A special officer for the railroad may welcome an opportunity to use his club on three or four young travelers. He will hesitate to attack twelve—or even three or four when he knows that they may return after dark with eight more. On the other hand, twenty or thirty child tramps challenge, through sheer numbers alone, the police and citizens. A jungle of but a dozen is let alone. A jungle of a hundred has to be well hidden to escape being raided every few days by the police.

This unit, like all tribal units, has at its head a chief. The chief owes his position to inherent gifts of leadership which show in a crisis. Quite often he is the largest and the strongest boy. Always he is the cleverest. Not always, however, is he the oldest. Boys of sixteen or seventeen often are leaders of gangs having members as old as twenty. The older boy may be thick-witted and lacking in leadership. When called upon he contributes his strength willingly as an ox and his fighting ability readily as a bulldog, but he leaves to his more intelligent comrades the outlining of plans and their execution. One quality the leader has without exception. That quality is courage. One quality the leader demands of his followers. That is loyalty.

The leader never asks of his followers something he will not do himself. When the stem is tough and his boys are hungry, he gets food. When the railroad police are hostile, he defies them. When his gang hesitates to board a fast down-grade freight, he does not hesitate. In all things at all times, he is the leader.

In return he insists upon loyalty. The boys must be loyal to him and to each cther. No chiseling, no holding out of food is allowed. The tribe is communistic. It shares its wealth with all its members. If one boy has luck today, and is able to steal some sausage or to beg some bread, he divides the food among all. Tomorrow somebody else may have luck.

But tomorrow somebody else may have luck and may chisel. What then? A tribe must have some method of enforcing its mandates. It may expel a member. It may beat a member. It may devise curious ways of expressing its disapproval of the individual's conduct. Young tramps use all of these methods. On the road the tribe can beat up or expel a member. In missions and relief stations the tribe is circumscribed, yet it still attempts to maintain control.

"Don't speak to Pete today," said Texas to me one morning in a mission. "We're giving him the silence."

"Why?"

"He hit the stem yesterday for some sausage and ate it all himself, and little Alf was hungry."

So they gave him the silence. All day we walked around ignoring Pete. When he spoke to us we did not answer. When he sat near us we paid no attention to him. When he looked at us we looked away. There were three hundred other men and boys in the mission. Pete was not lonesome. He talked to new arrivals. Yet he was hurt. He tried to attract our attention.

He tried to bribe one of the gang with a heel of rye bread and an onion. He tried to anger Texas and Dressy. But we gave him the silence.

For two days we did not speak to him. On the third, when we were leaving town, he followed us down into a reefer, and after four more hours of silence begged for mercy.

"If you guys will only speak to me I'll give you everything I got," he pleaded. "Honest to God, Tex, I never meant nothing by eating that bologna when Alf was hungry. I thought I was going back to the stem and get some more and then give it to him. I got only eleven cents, but you can have it all if you'll only speak to me, and the next burg we stop in, I'll hit the stem for all of you."

And he did. Pete was an efficient panhandler. Texas did not want to lose him. The silence was broken.

The tribe likes to travel as a group, occupying a box car and a jungle alone. The exigencies of transient life seldom permit this. New members are added; old ones are dropped. One week the group may be reduced to six; next week it may have eighteen or twenty. Yet in the vicissitudes of its transient existence the tribe tends to preserve its identity. Within the tribe there is division of labor. Jungle life exemplifies the division. In every tribe there are boys who are cooks, beggars, barbers, and thieves. The cooks prepare the food. The beggars go uptown to get it. The thieves get what the beggars cannot obtain. The barbers cut hair or repair clothing. And in the end all have a better meal than they would have without coöperation. Frequently this division is a sex division. The girls remain in camp while the boys hit the stem for groceries. Only about one tribe in five has female members. The other boys must learn to live without girls. And occasionally the girls are more efficient than the boys. They go with them on begging and prowling expeditions and supervise their work. Even in those camps, the girls do the cooking. Never have I seen a tribe where the girls went out and secured the food and the men remained at home and cooked it.

Some tribes are developing nocturnal habits. They sleep or travel by day, sleeping in box cars or brush jungles, and prowl by night. It is a good time to prowl. Police are less vigilant. Restaurants and bakeries are more generous after dark. Men on the street are more inclined to give a boy a dime. It is easier to board trains, raid gardens, search garbage cans, steal clothes, after nightfall.

Almost all gangs of boys and girls on the road have, as tribes have everywhere, a restricted geographical location. Young tramps, as well as older ones, tend to remain fairly close to the spot of their origin. Although driven away by want, they seldom go five hundred miles, and if they do, they soon return. Here within a circle the girls and boys lay out a route of missions, relief stations, jails, and jungles where they are sure of food and shelter for a day or two and where they can hit the main stem. They cover this route regularly. A gang of young tramps becoming adventurous may stray far afield, but generally they remain upon land which they know. Here they follow certain paths. They remain near means of transportation, railroads, highways, and best of all, junction centers where main lines cross. They establish jungles near water and seldom far from town. Generally they are on the sunny sides of hills with windbreaks west and north. A fuel supply—usually from a passing gondola or an adjacent grove—is near.

Just as some boys specialize in certain forms of begging, stealing, or promoting a racket, some tribes become specialized. Like attracts like, and, while there is division of labor within the tribe, there is specialization without. Some specialize merely in traveling; others in the different forms of stealing and begging. In a prowl, two boys act as scouts, one or two as lookouts, while another two do the heisting. One gang I knew made a practice of stealing milk bottles on Sunday mornings. They would arrive in town on Friday, look over the apartment and residential sections on Saturday, and "pick up" on Sunday morning. Another gang made a practice of breaking into garages, and a third of robbing parked cars. Armed with a piece of pipe and a dog chain they could twist a door handle off any car on a dark street and steal whatever it contained of value.

In fashioning the material they beg or steal, many

boys and girls approach genius. With a safety pin or a piece of wire they repair clothing, fix shoes, fasten the peak on a cap. Newspapers take the place of underwear, socks, and can be used to protect the head and ears. Boys fashion lean-tos out of whatever material is at hand, scrap tin, sheet iron, grain doors, and in the woods of dead timber. I have seen the boys make crude stone hatchets for pounding nails in shoes or driving stakes for a lean-to. Pete one day showed me how he carried a club up his sleeve to defend himself from dogs, and one girl wore pieces of birchbark inside her puttees for protection from dog bites. Boys use old grain or wheat sacks for sweaters or shirts by cutting three holes in them for arms and head. Razors and needles are the usual toilet articles carried by young tramps. One in ten may have a broken piece of comb; one in fifty a scissors. Almost all carry jackknives; a few a knapsack—or bindle.

The more experienced child tramps, however, travel light. They stuff an extra pair of socks into one pocket, a suit of underwear into the lining of a coat and, unencumbered, take the road. When clothes wear out they beg or steal new ones. When clothes accumulate, they are checked at a mission. There they remain for thirty days or six months until the boy returns. I have known young tramps who had clothes checked in half a dozen missions.

"I'm never any farther than a day away from a clean shirt," boasted Dressy. "I got clothes in every mission between Cleveland and St. Louis."

"Geez," regretted Boris, as he ripped the worn sole completely off a shoe dropping from a red ball "and I got a good pair parked in Minneapolis, but I guess I'll have to pay to get these fixed."

Every tribe, anthropologists tell us, has a distinctive language or dialect. The child tramps are rapidly developing one. Basically the language is English, with the addition of slang words and terms. Yet what foreigner using a grammar and the Oxford dictionary could understand!

"I'm on the fritz, see? And I carries the banner slinking harness bulls. Until glims. Then I batters private plunging like a gandy dancer and red bulls sock into the old heavy-foot himself. 'Tooting ringers for a scoffing?' he says. 'Come wid me, I'll give you a scoffing.' Skating on my uppers I mush talks him out of a hustle buggy ride and into mongee."

In English we would say:

"I was penniless. All night I walked the streets avoiding uniformed policemen until dawn. At which time I began door-to-door begging, walking rapidly as a steel worker walks on a beam, when without warning I encounter a detective. 'Are you begging for something to eat?' he says. 'Come with me and I'll give you something to eat.' Although I was in a precarious situation, I was able to convince him not to call the squad car but to feed me."

The purpose of language, of course, is to convey information to other members of the tribe. Another purpose is to prevent the uninitiated from divining your secrets and perhaps to talk to a friend without being understood by a listening spy. In Italy anti-Fascists are said to have adopted the habit of calling Mussolini simply "he." In much the same fashion boy tramps refer to welfare workers as "they." By the use of the pronoun they can discuss and criticize social workers and relief policies without fear. With the addition of their own slang terms, they can not only discuss but slander mission men in a mission and within their hearing.

The child tramps are not only developing a language of their own; they are concocting myths, as men around camp-fires have ever concocted them. There is, for instance, the child tramp who is a cross between Huckleberry Finn, the English Puck, and the German Eulenspiegel. A mischievous lad, he is, alway playing tricks. One of his tricks was to steal the engineer's dinner pail, the conductor's cap and the brakie's lantern on the same train. Another myth is the Wabash Cannonball—a phantom train, like the Flying Dutchman. This train is, of course, part of hobo legend, which includes such places as the sweet potato and rock candy mountains; the young tramps have merely modernized the tale. A third myth is one of a young girl with an insatiable sex appetite, who finally meets her match in a small strange lad who enters camp and agrees to bet his clothes he can satisfy her. Other myths tell of cruel railroad detectives and the hideous fate that eventually overtakes them, and of the father who drove his girl from home and wept when he found her dead.

It is difficult to know how much of this literature is original. The major part of it undoubtedly is inherited from old hobo narratives. What is interesting is that the young tramps have accepted and are passing on this literature which is definitely anti-Christian, anti-capitalistic, anti-feminine, and in its bitter portrayal of the life, anti-bum.

Like all tribes, the child tramps date their beginning from a definite crisis. In Genesis it is the creation of the world and the flood. The child tramps date their life from "before the big trouble came."

Enough has been said in the chapter on prestige standards to show the hierarchy from passenger stiffs, who never ride anything slower than the California Fruit Express, to camp scavengers, jungle buzzards, and the scum of all, the Jack-roller, who robs his fellow vagrants.

Every tribe enjoys seeing its numbers increase. The young tramps welcome the stranger. He is made to feel at home the second day, and after a few tests of courage and generosity he is admitted as a full member. Thereafter they will defend him, help him secure food or clothing, be as loyal to him in time of need as their life permits.

Religious, sex, and social life of their own the boys have, and a viewpoint on political organizations and society derived from their surroundings. Codes of honor and standards of right and wrong all are part of their new tribal life.

And interesting it is to know that if all knowledge and all material goods were swept away tomorrow, the boys and girls on the road would develop their own world and begin to build anew.

# XVI

VAGABONDAGE is as old as time and as universal as air. The child tramps of America differ in degree but not in kind from the wild boys of Russia and the free youth of Germany after the war, the child tramps of Italy during the Austrian invasion a hundred years ago, or the present bands of Chinese boys turned pirate. Wherever there is social chaos there are homeless wanderers. And of these homeless wanderers a large number in all times and all places must be boys, some will be girls. The older men and women fail in their task of governing. There is invasion from without; revolution from within; or, as in our country, a complete breakdown of the mechanism of exchange and production. And men, women, and children take to the road and their chance.

Let us, for the sake of historical perspective, glance over some of these major movements in the past. At present there is in some quarters a disposition to blame the machine for everything. And yet in pre-machine days, there was vagabondage.

In the first general strike in history, the Jews walked out on Pharaoh, leaving Egypt and its fleshpots, and wandering for forty years in the wilderness. In Greece

221

slaves ran away from masters, as they always have, and, for the first time, a new class of vagabonds appeared— men who were not slaves but free citizens, soldiers crippled in the Peloponnesian Wars, brokers ruined in speculation, petty landowners expropriated by creditors, and small business men forced out by stronger competitors. They were citizens of Greece, but penniless. Different ways were tried of dealing with them and with the slaves. The slaves were pursued and punished; the ex-soldiers were given special privileges. One of these privileges was peddling without a license. An English poet gives us a pathetic picture of an ex-hero now reduced to canvassing in Athens.

> "Weak words he has that slip the nerveless tongue
> Deformed like his great frame; a broken arc:
> Once radiant as the javelin flung
> Right at the center breast-plate of his mark."

But everybody could not peddle. The number of tramps and vagabonds increased. Greece tried to repress them. The Laws of Lycurgus, the Codes of Draco and of Solon, all made vagabondage a felony punishable by torture and death. A tramp caught on the highways or in the woods became the property of the man catching him. If he attempted to escape a second time, he could be branded, suffer amputation of an arm or leg, or be agonizingly put to death.

Rome, too, had its vagabonds. Africa, England, Spain, and Mesopotamia furnished the conquering Empire with millions of slaves. At first there was room for all. With Roman men away fighting or at home and at ease, the Empire could use a large slave population. There came a day, however, when even luxury-loving Rome could absorb no more slave labor. The market became glutted. Roman industrialists, like their American prototypes, wished to reduce the burden of caring for marginal labor. Here we lay men off. The Romans were more clever. They invented manumission, the freeing of old and economically unproductive slaves. Cast out in his old age, from the household which he had enriched by his labors, the unfortunate man was thrown upon the state for a living with the other free but penniless Roman citizens. In addition to manumitted slaves, this class comprised ex-soldiers, small ruined merchants, tenant farmers forced to the wall by big landholders, and thousands of men dispossessed by mortgagors who during every depression gobbled up the land and homes of Romans, even as is being done today. The men drifted to Rome and other cities of the Empire. There the relief policies were not unlike our own. Nobody starves, we say today, and we dole out food. The Romans gave free grain. Bread and circuses was the policy of Rome. Ours is only bread.

But men need more than bread. They need occupations, for without occupations they become vagabonds.

In dealing with vagabonds, Rome followed the repressive policies of Greece. Vagabonds, if young and workable, were captured and returned to slavery. If old and unworkable, they were branded or marked by having ears clipped, noses slit, or fingers chopped away one at a time and cast into a fire before their eyes. Past masters in the art of controlling subjects through the judicious use of fear, Rome improved upon its predecessor's policies. Crucifixion was a favorite device. Vagabonds could be crucified at the crossroads where they were captured. If runaway slaves, they could be returned to their master and crucified in the slave quarters, where they would be left decomposing for days while crows fed upon their flesh and men turned their heads aside in horror from a scene of shame.

And yet in spite of all its cruelty and terror, in spite of all its crucifixions and mutilations, Rome could not repress its vagabonds. More than a little they contributed to the fall of the once eternal city. For two hundred years before Alaric sacked the city, wealthy citizens went to bed at night in fear of an uprising of the vagabonds and slaves, and it was the city's vagabonds and slaves more than Alaric's military power that opened the gates never before opened to a conqueror.

Following the collapse of Rome, and the barbarian invasion, half the population of Western Europe became vagabonds. Roaming bands of armed men infested the countryside, pillaged cities, waylaid travelers. Out of this confusion, insecurity, and barbarism arose strong men, walled cities, and the institution of feudalism. With all its defects, feudalism gave stability to society and protection to the individual. Serfs, it is true, were tied to the manor lord, but the manor lord was tied to the serfs. The men could not be cast off to become vagabonds.

Vagabondage was a privilege which the nobility reserved for themselves. Clad in armor, they traveled from castle to castle, ostensibly keeping the highways free from robbers and rescuing beautiful maidens from cruel ogres, but actually having a grand time enjoying their friends' hospitality.

Into this stratified society with its knights in armor, its Parliaments of Love, and its mild internecine warfare came the Crusades. Of all the dynamic movements in Western Europe from the Fall of Rome to the discovery of America, the Crusades were the greatest. With no whip of technological invention, no spur of civil war, no spark of revolutionary gun-powder to initiate them, the Crusades, like Minerva, sprang full-armed into the world. There was Peter the Hermit, and the Legend of the Holy Grail, and the heathen who had seized the tomb of Christ.

And that was all.

Yet soon in a thousand villages men were enlisting for service in the East, in a thousand armories steel was being forged into swords and bucklers, in a thousand courtyards stout horses were being trained in the maneuvers of battle. For the next two hundred years the population movement was eastward. But the Mussulman became too strong. He recaptured Jerusalem.

Acre fell. Even the powerful citadel of the Knights Templar surrendered. The Crusaders returned.

And with their return came vagabonds by the millions. It is impossible to estimate the amount of aimless tramping that occurred coincidental with and following the Crusades. Bands of armed men marched south in the van of bona fide Crusaders and claimed hospitality as their just dues, for were they not on their way to fight the heathen? Later the same band, asserting they had been to Syria, marched north. Again they claimed and received hospitality in return for tales of adventures they had never had and battles they had never fought. When the Crusaders were demobilized thousands joined these wandering bands. Vagabondage became a pestilence.

And a pestilence cured it. The Black Death brought back by the Crusaders spread over Europe, and depopulated the land, falling upon the hewers of wood and the drawers of water as well as on the vagabonds of the road and the thieves of the forest. When the plague had run its course, the old vagrants were gone—and with them a substantial portion of the adult population.

Yet not even the Black Death could long cure Europe of the affliction of men on the bum. Feudal society was beginning to disintegrate; bourgeois society to rise. From now on, in both contemporary literature and historical documents, we find evidence of vagabonds. There is Spanish picaresque literature and its romances of Lope de Vega. There are the ballads of Robin Hood and his Merry Men, and the free foresters of Germany. There is the first armed revolt of vagabonds in England. In 1347 bands of these men overran the country north of the Severn. In Gloucestershire they joined together and elected a chief, and setting at defiance the king and his laws, infested the land and the sea. It required an army to quell them. There were, too, the teachings and practices of the Church. Christians were urged to give charity to the poor, to harbor the harborless and to shelter the shelterless. Monasteries were open at all times for the relief of travelers. Extra buildings were provided for their care. Monks were to see that they were liberally entertained and that they behaved themselves with proper decorum. And the number of vagabonds increased, until when Wat Tyler recruited his desperate band for the first uprising of the proletariat in English history, England in proportion to its population had five times as many wanderers as America has today. Later in the days of Elizabeth and the enclosures "it seemed that every second man one met on the highway was a vagabond, and every fifth family in the nation was homeless and wandering."

Different methods for treating vagabondage were devised. None was successful. Since we derive most of our legal concepts and many of our social institutions from England, it may be well for us to review that nation's experience.

From the days of King Canute—he who attempted to still the tides—in 1017 we find laws dealing with vagabonds. Each successive law was more rigorous than its predecessor, but the act of Edward VI in 1547 was the most cruel.

It read in part:

"Forasmuch as Idleness and Vagabundry is the mother and roote of all theftes, robbryes and all evill actes and other mischief and the multitude of people given thereto hath allwaies been here within this realm verie greate . . . every person loytering and wandering not seeking worke or leaving it when engaged . . . shall be taken up before the Justices of the Peace . . . who shall immediately cause the said loyterer to be marked with a whott iron in the brest the mark V and adjudge the said personne living so Idelye to such Presenter to be his slave. . . ."

The slave is to be fed bread and water or small drink and such refuse meats as the master thinks fit. He is to be caused to work by beating, chaining, or otherwise in whatever work he may be put to, however vile it may be. If he runs away his master may pursue and punish him. If he runs away a second time he may be put to death.

The reign of Edward VI marks the nadir in cruelty for English-speaking nations in handling a helpless and hapless race of unfortunates whose only crime was their poverty. From then on, England's policy became more lenient.

Lenient, but not soft, became the policy of Albion.

The following Rules from a House of Correction in the seventeenth century appear strict enough:

". . . all constables are to carry all idle persons to the house. . . . It is ordered that every stronge or sturdie roag at his or her first enterance . . . shall have XIIL stripe upon his beare skynne . . . and that every yong roag or idle loyterrer have VI stripe and that every one withoute fayle . . . shall have put upon him . . . some clogge, chaine, collars of iron, ringlet, or manacle . . . the whips shall be made with cords withoute knottes, and the partie that shall receive the punishment shall have his or her clothes turned of their shoulders to the beare skynne down to the waste. . . ."

And, strange as it may seem to those who feel that "we are too good to our old bums anyway," this policy was not successful. In spite of whips and chains and red whott irons, vagabondage in England increased.

The best statement of what was wrong with England's vagrancy laws is contained in a tract written by one Mr. Stanley, a reformed vagabond, to His Majesty, James I, King of England and the British Isles. The "lawes against idyle loyterers" had been modified somewhat. The counselors of James proposed to restore them in all their pristine rigor and severity. Mr. Stanley wrote in protest against the suggested legislation. He petitioned, in part, as follows:

". . . For the general rule of England is to whip and punish the wandering beggars and to brand them according to the new law, and so mark them with a note of infamie, as they may be assured no man will set them to work.  And so many Justices do practice one branch of that good Statute which is the point of justice, but as for the point of Charity they leave undone which is to provide houses and convenient places to set the poore to work which ought to be done in equity and justice.

"The poor may be whipped to death and branded as roags and so become felons by Law and next time hanged for vagrancy and no private man will put them to work. . . .

"The right and interest of punishing Roags is but the destruction of vices and the saving of men. . . . The law commands that the Vagrants should repair to the place where they were born or last dwelled. . . . There are thousands of these people that their place of birth is utterly unknowne and that they never had any abiding place in their lives. . . .

". . . It is very lamentable that Poore Roags and Beggars should be whipped and branded according to the law and otherwise punished because they are begging or idle when no place is provided to set them to work . . . surely many would go to the workhouse to work if such houses were provided for them. . . . Tell the begging souldier and the wandering sturdie beggar that they are able to work for their living and bid them go to work and they will presently answer you that they would work if they could get it. . . ."

King James, however, was not to rule long, nor was he to follow Mr. Stanley's sensible suggestion.  The number of unemployed and vagrant increased in the kingdom to be cleared away only by the Civil Wars of Cromwell. The petition of Mr. Stanley, however, was not written in vain. It called attention to the fundamental weakness of England's vagrancy laws. From his time on, Parliament concerned itself not only with apprehending and punishing vagabonds but with providing workhouses and work.

It is not useful to trace the history of English poor relief further. England had outlets for vagrants denied us at present. In addition her policy of colonial expansion, indenturing servants, impressing sailors, exiling all kinds of malefactors to Baffin Bay, Van Diemen's Land, and other places in Australia kept vagabondage down at home. The commercial growth of the nation following the success of her colonizing projects offered work for all in the factories of Sheffield and Birmingham, the mines of Cornwall, and the shipyards of the Clyde and the Mersey.

The same policy of expansion kept vagabondage down in America. For one hundred years, we had a constantly expanding frontier. A man out of work or a boy without a home could go West, settle on free land, and in the course of time become prosperous. Our first wave of vagrants came when Jefferson passed the Embargo Act in an effort to avoid foreign entanglements in the Napoleonic Wars of England and France. Thousands of sailors were thrown out of work. It was a simple matter for them to cross the Appalachians as westward the frontier pushed. Strictly speaking, for the first hundred years of our history there was no vagrancy problem. The problem was to supply enough men to meet the demands of the never-satisfied labor market.

The construction of canals, the grading of post roads, and especially the building of the Baltimore and Ohio Railroad created temporary problems of vagrancy. The job over, great numbers of single men were released to wander over and to prey upon the countryside. The Civil War and the West with its alluring frontier took up the men. Vagrancy became no problem until after the Civil War. Thousands of men, many maimed in the war, wandered through the land. Repressive laws were enacted; special land grants were given to soldiers. New precious metals were discovered in Nevada, Arizona, and Colorado. Transcontinental railroad construction began, demanding men and more men.

And then one day thirty or forty years ago, the railroads were built. Ribbons of steel traversed the desert, penetrated mountains, sprang across rivers and an American epic was over. Thousands of men were unemployed when the Union Pacific and Southern Pacific systems had been completed. The land in the Southwest open to settlement was mostly sub-marginal. Large cattle ranches monopolized the arable tracts. On the other pieces a very inferior grade of wheat, almost worthless to millers in those days, was grown. Gambling joints and saloons, usually financed by the contractors or railroad companies, had acquired the men's wages.

Penniless and begging their way, the men came East
and North. When asked where they were from or where
they worked, they replied, "The Panhandle," using the
name of a part of Texas for the whole railroad system
in the Southwest. From this we get the term "panhandler," meaning an able-bodied man who is a beggar.
In the North conditions were somewhat different. The
completion of the northern railroad systems released
thousands of men as had been the case in the South, but
other industries absorbed them. Lumber and flour mills,
factories and mines, smelters and shops needed men in
great numbers. The rise of the automobile industry and
its necessary corollary, highway construction, the war-
time spurt of all business, the post-war boom in building
and foreign trade practically eliminated the tramp as a
poverty problem. Only men obviously unemployable
were unemployed for more than a few months during
the decade of 1918-1928.

Yet even during our best days we had a form of
vagabondage that contributed not a little to the present
problem. Expanding cities such as Detroit, boom states
such as Florida, transient industries such as power line
and dam construction—all these demanded mobile labor. Michigan factories sucked men from California,
California road camps lured men from Iowa, Florida
construction drew men from New York, and New York
drew men from all over the country. We prided ourselves upon the mobility of our labor. Economists told
us that it was a source of natural wealth not unlike water

power or mines. Labor traveled in day coaches, in flivvers, on work tickets, on its own money, but labor traveled. And in traveling labor dissipated much of its earnings, lost home-making habits, and acquired the mental outlook of vagabondia. Today we are paying for the mobility of labor during the last decade, and we may continue to pay for years to come.

# XVII

IT is well, indeed, to consider the experience of the past. For after all the story of vagabondage is, in the history of the race, an old, old story. There is danger, if we look upon the boy tramps of America as being entirely the product of the machine age and social disintegration of our times, of losing perspective and giving way to blank discouragement and despair. Yet nations in times past have had vagabonds and have lived. We, too, will endure in spite of an army of boy and girl tramps on the loose.

We will endure, but only if we face the problem intelligently. We must consider it not only in the light of history, but of our own complex machine age.

Already there is in some quarters a disposition to treat the homeless man as a deliberate and uncompromising bum, and the boy tramp as a national menace. We forget that during the days of employment there were few homeless men, fewer bums, and no boy or girl tramps. When work was plentiful, men worked. Now there is no work. Families are broken. Homes are destroyed. Unemployed men wander from state to state and from city to city in search of a job and bread. We do not know what to do about them. An-

gered at our own social inefficiency, we turn our spleen
against the men and assert, "Nine out of ten of those
men wouldn't work if you offered them a job." And
we forget that we have no job to offer even the tenth
man.

Toward the child tramps we have, until recently,
adopted an ostrich policy. Occasionally we raise our
head from its hole, glance about bewildered and hys-
terical, make a few ineffectual squawks of sympathy,
and once more hide in the sand. Yet every day, more
youths are taking to the road, and every day more boy
and girl tramps are graduating into the ranks of adult
and chronic transients.

The Civilian Conservation Corps has done little to
check the exodus of children. It enlists only boys and
not all of them. To be eligible a youth must be
eighteen. Fully half the boys and girls on the road are
younger. He must have dependents, a residence, and
a reference. Many of the boys lack more than dependents. They lack a home. Others have been on the
road so long they no longer can claim any place as
residence. The only reference they can give would be
a police record. Furthermore, the corps is a forestry
conservation corps interested primarily in saving our
forests. What we need is a new Child Conservation
Corps which will have as its purpose the saving not of
our forests a hundred years from today, but of our boys
and girls growing into the men and women of tomorrow.

The new transient detention camps, like the forestry

corps, tend to be one-sex and adult camps. Their primary purpose is to reduce adult vagrancy and provide
a place for homeless men and women to stay. They
make it unnecessary for the adult vagrant to wander
from state to state, but by assuring him of a place where
he can rest and recuperate, receive good food and medical attention any time he desires, they may encourage
vagrancy even as the monasteries in the Middle Ages
encouraged it. On the boys and girls in box cars they
may have no effect whatever. They may force them
to avoid missions, welfare stations, and police even more
than the youngsters are avoiding them now. Yet they
are a step in the right direction and one which we must
take if we are ever to reduce the number of transients
in our country. For, I repeat, we need a place not only
where we can restrain the adult bum, but where we
can permit the young transient to develop and to grow
into a useful citizen.

What we need precisely is a national plan of youth
camps not unlike the youth camps in Europe. For
while the problem of wandering youth is new in
America it is old in Europe, and although Europe has
not solved it, methods of minimizing the evil effects
of vagrancy have been worked out.

These methods do not attempt—as we are attempting—to force youths to remain at home when there is
in the true sense of the word no home in which they
can remain. After the war almost every home in Germany was clothed in anguish and despair. Youth tried

to escape from the homes ruined by the war even as our own youth is trying to escape from homes ruined by the depression. It took to the road. Bands of wandering boys and girls roved the countryside. In Germany inexpensive summer camps were established for them. The purpose of the camps is to develop the bodies and personalities of the youths. Setting-up exercises are a part of daily routine. Games, contests, plays, community singing, debating, all belong to the camp life. There are libraries, a discussion hall, special lectures, health and psychiatric clinics. Part of the day is spent in manual labor, part in study and discussion, part in recreation and play. The morale of youth is maintained. Its potentialities are increased through learning and labor.

The camps are maintained by the state for the youths. Youths living in a camp are segregated from the deleterious influences of broken homes and of old men who have failed in life. They are surrounded by an atmosphere of optimism and effort. For thirty hours a week they work at manual labor. They construct some permanent improvement for the state which all may enjoy. Hiking paths through mountains, recreational centers in towns, state parks, a series of resthouses and dining halls for picnic parties have all been built or improved by youths working in camps. The work must not compete with regular labor. The improvement must be one which could not have been made had regular labor been used.

And in the end youths are maintained in or restored to physical strength and mental vigor and the state has a permanent improvement—all at no greater cost than would be required to keep youths on a dole in misery and squalor and at a cost less perhaps than we in America have been paying to shunt youth from town to town and to force them more and more into permanent vagabondia.

Although the youth movement in Germany has been best known and the youth organizations in Russia best publicized, almost every nation in Europe has been faced with the problem and has solved it the same way. Work or subsistence camps for students and other youths have been established in Switzerland, Austria, Italy, France, Belgium, and England. And in all countries the camps have been successful.

They have been successful, but they have not remade the world. We must be careful and not become overly enthusiastic about camp life. After all, camp life is but training for camp life and if unwisely continued may result in maladjustment for the individual when he leaves the camp. We need more than training for camp life. We need training for a complex social life and an understanding of man, his problems and possibilities.

Perhaps one of the best ways in which we could furnish youth with this opportunity would be to initiate a colonization project for youth on land now unused. We have in the valleys of Alaska and our Western and Southern states idle land which can be converted into fertile fields, rivers to furnish power, mines for steel and coal, to build community industrial centers where youth could live in self-sustained independence. Under vigorous leadership, the boys and girls today becoming vagabonds could be mobilized into work armies to build power and irrigation dams, highways, ditches, apartment houses, recreational centers, and all the equipment needed for self-supporting self-contained coöperative community. Here they would grow their own food, make their own clothing, build their own houses, and receive training that would fit them for a life of self-respect no matter where they lived.

At present the boys and girls on the road certainly are not getting training for life. Men may live again as nomads and hunters of the forest. If they do, the child tramps are being prepared for that life. American cities may be overrun with groups of hoodlums and depredators, as London was in the eighteenth and Paris in the seventeenth century, forcing the honest citizen to remain in his domicile after dark or proceed abroad under escort and at the risk of physical combat. If they are, today's child tramps will supply many recruits for the new army. Street beggars, hideous, deformed, and depressing, may swarm our land and deface our cities and again many of them will be graduate child tramps.

Optimists, it is true, see in the life of the boys some advantages. Wishing to apologize for the present mess and to justify the ways of mammon to man, they assert that the boys are learning independence, self-reliance, and the whole gamut of ancient virtues which made this country what it is today. One social work executive has asserted that they are carrying on the glorious tradition of American life and extending the frontier. Another relief official has asserted that road life may be good for a lad. It toughens him. Which brings to mind the kind-hearted employer in Dickens who built a fire under little sweeps, stuck in a chimney, for then they would struggle more to extricate themselves.

Yet I, who have lived with the child tramps, eaten with them, slept with them, studied them for two years, find little that is wholesome and nothing that is permanently good. It is encouraging, I admit, but not surprising to learn that the child tramps, left to themselves and living as outcasts of society, develop rules and regulations, elect leaders, and enforce their punishments without the aid of elders.

It is not encouraging, however, to see the youth of our land spend their days in idleness and the acquiring of habits definitely anti-social. For this new tribal life of the boys is opposed to all concepts of society not only as we know it but as it must be in the future if we are to progress. Men may again retreat to caves or squat like gypsies around a campfire. They may mutilate themselves with conch shells and stain the wounds with wode while chanting strange voodoo songs among the canebrake. But it is not likely.

Nor is it likely that America will ever again need a great army of casual laborers similar to the hoboes of a generation past. These men were the logical successors to the woodsmen and plainsmen of a hundred years before. To push back the industrial frontier was their task. They lived lives of useful, if at times riotous, toil. American industrialism was then at its most expansive and adventurous period. It was the hobo's job to go West where remote and far-flung enterprises were being built by men who had no steady homes. Such undertakings called for laborers who were glad to toil manfully for a while in inaccessible regions, celebrate the completion of the task in a week of booze and riots and then be on their way to a new job. The work itself was dull and prosaic, but the men satisfied their adventurous spirit by varying jobs and undergoing hardships in new, strange places. Their toil built the railroads, sunk shafts for mines, drilled oil wells, felled trees, dammed rivers, dug irrigation ditches, constructed power dams, raised cattle and sheep in new, raw regions where the settled family man could not go.

Such was the hobo of old. He was no romantic, rollicking vagabond roving merrily and loving as he roved. Nor was he a wandering beggar, an evil-looking tramp who labored only on compulsion. He was an honest working man. The place he filled in the industrial development of our country was one of high worth and should be honored.

The place that the child tramps can fill if they continue

their present life is one of little worth and no honor. We have no need of a maverick army of casual laborers. The West is no longer free. The frontier is but a memory. Machines build our highways, garner our grain, extend the industrial line. And other work is concentrated in centralized communities requiring steady citizens. There is today no need for a vast army of casuals.

There is even less need for an army that is merely migrating. For the hobo of old tended to become a nuisance after he had completed his work. When the railroads were all built, when the West was settled and flourishing, when age and rheumatism had claimed their due, he turned back East and became a pest to friends or a burden to society. Still, if he finished his life a dependent or a bum, he had in his time been a useful citizen. Today's child tramp is beginning his life a vagrant. In the natural course of time, he will finish it a street beggar or a jailbird.

And such an end for a whole army of American youth will be occasion for more than regret, more than a bitter sorrow. It will be cause for despair. Better for them and for our nation if they rode into the valley of death and perished upon the field of honor in the most stupid war that history has ever recorded. We have more youth on the road than France has to call to the colors this year or than we lost in the last war. In days past we prided ourselves upon what we were doing not only for our own youth, but for the youth of all nations. Yet in the crisis we are sublimely doing nothing.

While other nations are building up their youth, we are permitting economic conditions to tear ours down. Russia, Italy, Germany and Japan have intensive policies and programs for their youth. France, England, and the Scandinavian countries lag not far behind. Only China, the United States, and perhaps a few backward revolt-torn South American countries are standing aside while the wolves of chance take the children.

The problem, I admit, is not simple. America is still in a depression. The families of the boys, where families exist, cannot take care of them. Industry has little enough work for experienced, competent men and none at all for immature youths. Schools with budgets cut and terms shortened cannot assume new burdens. We are no military nation demanding a large standing army. Over a quarter of a million boys and girls are on the road. Work camps are but expedients. They cannot solve the problem.

The camps, as I have said, are but expedients. They will save today's youth from vagabondage; they will create public works of use and value; they will give us a pause during which we can prepare a better program, but still they are only expedients. Unless we are to become a militaristic or monastic nation we cannot confine our youth permanently in camps. The camps will save the boys on the road today, but for tomorrow we must have other and more comprehensive programs.

And for these it will be necessary to examine not only our present policies of handling youth but our entire economic and social system, the philosophy and practices of which have driven youth into vagabondage.

For what precisely are we living? To get rich? To make the world safe for democracy? To help Germany pay its war debt and to rebuild? To keep Japan from stepping on China's neck? To prevent Europe from enjoying another war? Yet a good deal of our energies in the last decade have been expended in the interests of these and similar ideals. With a national messianic complex, we have attempted to manage and reform other people's business. We built railroads in South America, dug mines in Africa, constructed model tenements in Vienna.

Only recently, with 10,000,000 men in need of clothing and 5,000,000 children in rags, we gave cotton to China, cotton which the wise Chinese immediately sold to Japan at a profit. And today we are contemplating the giving of machines and materials to Russia in order that Russia's youth may be well-clad and well-fed while our own go hungry and in want. For while we were caring for other people's children, our own were in rags.

To reclaim the youth which we are losing will not be easy. It will require more than a namby-pamby policy of additional recreational centers and greater choice of high school subjects. It will require more than the voicing of lofty sentiments and the passing of pious resolutions of hope. It will require a redirection of national aims and ideals into a future in which youth will have a definite part.

Since the closing of the frontier American youth has been exploited, neglected, or frustrated. It has been exploited first by child labor employers and second by schools. Without any consistent social or national point of view, the schools in general have regarded the younger generation as an oyster. Parents, wishing to be relieved of responsibility, have neglected children under the sophistry that they were aiding them in self-development and the expression of individuality. Youth without the leadership and direction it required or the knowledge and strength it needed became bored with a life devoid of plan or purpose. In the post-war days of prosperity and gin, it expressed its frustration in drink and sexual promiscuity. Today it expresses its frustration in wandering on the road.

Tomorrow American youth must be led. It must be led by men who know where they are going, where the country is going, and where they want youth to go.

And in this new country not only will the beasts of the field have their lairs and the wild birds their nests, but every child will have a home insured from economic disaster, and there will be no youthful wanderers cold and hungry sleeping without even a gypsy's tent between them and the sky.

# APPENDIX

WHILE it may be true that the literary method of portraying new and strange aspects of social life is superior in certain respects to the scientific method, it has its limitations. Not every observer will report the same things. Emotion may enter and color some details. Unconscious propaganda and prejudice may be present. Still, I insist, it is the only acceptable method for ascertaining a complete and true picture in many fields. If we could have a complete and true record of marriages, if a trained observer could live as intimately with a series of married couples over a period of years as I lived with the boys and girls on the road, taking not only day by day but hourly notes, he could give us a true picture of marital relations only by using a literary approach. It would be essential, however, that the observer collect facts in systematic and orderly manner and subordinate artistic impulse to the preponderance of scientific fact. Then, even if not one actual fact occurred exactly as given, he would still be presenting a truer picture than he could through the use of any other method. Too often in the past have we relied upon the facts of one case history (which may not be typical and may not be complete in all details) or upon tabular presentation of material gathered through the use of a questionnaire or a formal interview in which the person interviewed knew he was being interviewed and in which he reacted according to the demands of the social situation. We need a new technique in sociology, one which will unite the training and methods of science with the tools of literature and produce a picture that will result in a better understanding of society than we now have.

It will be necessary for the scientist to maintain the scientific point of view in his investigation and to search, not for literary material as the journalist does but for facts upon which he can base conclusions expressed in an artistic fashion. Into this conceptual framework he will merge facts collected on the basis of scientific hypothesis. From the viewpoint of science he will lose nothing, for his work will have been done according to standards and techniques which, while tending to become personal as all professional skill becomes personal, may nevertheless be duplicated by anybody who will subject himself to the discipline. New techniques will have to be evolved for new situations, but that is a part of the scientist's task.

Facts in regard to the young tramps are needed in order to arrive at an intelligent understanding of the problem. The facts used here were collected in jungles, box cars, and missions, according to techniques developed in my thesis study of the attitudes of transient men and boys. In no case did the boy or girl know that he or she was giving me material. We sat down and talked, or walked along the railroad tracks, and they told me something about themselves. I put the facts down in writing as soon as possible. Those who are interested in a theoretical discussion and a description of this phase of this problem are referred to my thesis.

The first important fact to note is the number of case histories, and the number of interviews. Case histories are complete life stories. Interviews are merely discussions in which I collected some information in regard to the young tramp, but not enough for a complete case history. The total number of interviews, for both boys and girls, equals 1465 of whom 1377 were boys and 88 girls. Case histories were collected for 493 boys, 16 girls; interviews were made with 884 boys and 72 girls. Table I.

The next fact that we notice is the number of native and foreign-born and the place of their birth. Table II. The place of birth of parents is next shown. Table III.

Continuing our study of the origins of the young tramps, we find that the boys came from many states and large cities chiefly in the industrial East. Tables IV and V.

The next important factor is the age distribution. Table VI. The median age is 16.94. The age of this group study must not be taken as indicative of the ages of all transients.  A true picture of all transients would not show a bulge in the middle of the curve at 17 but a gradual rise from the lower age level to about 30 and then a tapering off to old age.  There are on the road more transients between 18 and 21 than Table VI indicates.  I did not interview this older group for my study.  Boys and girls over 18 tend to leave the younger groups and to associate with adult transients.  For this study I interviewed only those who lived as youthful vagrants.

Religious sects and Protestant denominations are shown in Tables VII and VIII.  A curious fact and one worth noting is that non-believers represent the second most populous group and that many of the more important Protestant sects are not represented at all.

Parental status in the home is worth study.  After all, there is no point to sending the youths home if they have no homes.  Table IX.  The small number of complete homes, 176, suggests that even before the depression the young tramps lived in homes that were marginal.  Death rather than divorce has been the greatest divider of child tramps' homes, and separation has counted but little.  The incidence of multiple divorce, however, is interesting as suggesting not only the break-up of homes, but the possibility of parental emotional instability which might have been transferred to the child through environment or the blood stream.  The surprising number who admit illegitimate birth is strange.  It is not impossible that the figure is too high and that more than one boy and girl expressed his or her dissatisfaction with parents by disowning them. The youth felt perhaps that his parents had failed or rejected him, and he in turn rejected them.

The number of orphans exceeds the number of illegitimate children. The presence of a step-parent in so many homes is of no significance when compared with the number of homes in which there could have been a step-parent, although in some case histories the part of a step-parent appears important as a factor in forcing the child on the road.

Sibling position, Table X, is of only minor importance. Children of divorce were frequently the only children.

The family employment situation as shown in Table XI gives us a picture of a home badgered by want. The father was unemployed in 254 homes at the time the boy or girl ran away, and in 61 homes the father and at least one other wage-earning brother or sister were out of work. The period of parental unemployment before the boy or girl left home is shown in Table XII.

Table XIII shows why the boys and girls left home. Table XIV shows how long they have been on the road. Tables XV and XVI give more data on the family situation which might help to explain why the boys or girls took to the road.

Table XVII reveals some educational retardation and corroborates other information. Boys and girls on the road are underprivileged. The small number, Table

XVIII, who participated in Scout and other activities verifies the hypothesis of poverty and underprivilege.

Obvious physical defects, conditions of shoes and clothing are shown in Table XIX.

Facts in regard to the young migrants are necessary in order to have an intelligent comprehension of the subject. Legislation based upon incomplete or inaccurate data may be more harmful than good. The present investigation has unearthed some facts. More are needed.

TABLE I—NUMBER OF YOUNG TRAMPS INTERVIEWED
NUMBER OF CASE HISTORIES COLLECTED BY SEX

|  | Boys | Girls |
|---|---|---|
| TOTAL | 1377 | 88 |
| Interviews | 884 | 72 |
| Case histories | 493 | 16 |

TABLE II—NATIVITY OF 493 BOYS AND 16 GIRL TRAMPS

| Country | Boys | Girls |
|---|---|---|
| TOTAL | 493 | 16 |
| United States | 472 | 13 |
| Italy | 5 | 1 |
| Hungary | 3 | |
| Jugoslavia | 3 | 1 |
| Sweden | 2 | 1 |
| Armenia | 2 | |
| Russia | 2 | |
| Bulgaria | 1 | |
| Germany | 1 | |
| Poland | 1 | |
| Lithuania | 1 | |

### TABLE III—BIRTHPLACE OF PARENTS OF 493 BOY AND 16 GIRL TRAMPS

| Nation | Boys | Girls |
|---|---|---|
| TOTAL | 493 | 16 |
| United States | 372 | 9 |
| Russia: | | |
|    Jews | 18 | 2 |
|    Other Russians | 8 | |
| Italy | 16 | 2 |
| Germany | 16 | |
| Poland | 11 | |
| Sweden | 9 | 1 |
| Jugoslavia | 9 | 1 |
| Hungary | 8 | |
| Armenia | 7 | |
| Czechoslovakia | 6 | 1 |
| Finland | 4 | |
| Ireland | 3 | |
| Austria | 2 | |
| Bulgaria | 1 | |
| Norway | 1 | |
| Lithuania | 1 | |
| French Canadian | 1 | |

TABLE IV—HOME STATE OF 493 BOY AND 16 GIRL TRAMPS

| State | Boys | Girls |
|---|---|---|
| TOTAL | 493 | 16 |
| Pennsylvania | 52 | 3 |
| Michigan | 48 | 1 |
| Ohio | 45 | |
| New York | 40 | 2 |
| Texas | 39 | |
| Illinois | 30 | |
| Indiana | 28 | 1 |
| California | 24 | 5 |
| Wisconsin | 20 | 2 |
| Kentucky | 20 | |
| Missouri | 19 | |
| Tennessee | 19 | 1 |
| Nebraska | 16 | |
| Washington | 12 | |
| Iowa | 14 | |
| North Dakota | 12 | |
| Minnesota | 11 | 1 |
| Georgia | 10 | |
| Rhode Island | 9 | |
| Arizona | 8 | |
| Wyoming | 6 | |
| Oregon | 3 | |
| All other states | 8 | |

TABLE V—PRINCIPAL CITIES IN WHICH BOY AND GIRL
TRAMPS FORMERLY LIVED

| City | Boys | Girls |
|---|---|---|
| TOTAL ......................... | 98 | 5 |
| Philadelphia ....................... | 21 | |
| Chicago .......................... | 20 | 2 |
| Detroit ........................... | 18 | 1 |
| New York ........................ | 18 | |
| Cleveland ......................... | 6 | 1 |
| St. Louis ......................... | 5 | |
| Memphis ......................... | 4 | 1 |
| Los Angeles ....................... | 3 | |
| Houston .......................... | 3 | |

TABLE VI—AGE DISTRIBUTION OF 548 BOY AND GIRL
TRAMPS

| Age | Boys | Girls |
|---|---|---|
| TOTAL ......................... | 548 | 29 |
| Less than 13 ...................... | 3 | 1 |
| 13, less than 15 ................... | 78 | 9 |
| 15, less than 17 ................... | 191 | 13 |
| 17, less than 19 ................... | 153 | 6 |
| 19, less than 21 ................... | 94 | 0 |
| 21 ............................... | 29 | 0 |

TABLE VII—RELIGION OF 402 BOY AND 11 GIRL TRAMPS

| Religion | Boys | Girls |
|----------|------|-------|
| TOTAL ........................ | 402 | 11 |
| Protestant ...................... | 264 | 3 |
| Catholics ...................... .. | 52 | 1 |
| Jews ........................... | 24 | 0 |
| Non-Believers ................... | 62 | 7 |

TABLE VIII—DENOMINATIONAL CHURCH OF 237 PROTESTANT
YOUNG TRAMPS

| Denomination | Number |
|--------------|--------|
| TOTAL ................................. | 247 |
| Methodist ............................... | 81 |
| Baptist ................................. | 63 |
| Lutheran ................................ | 54 |
| Congregationalist ......................... | 11 |
| Quaker ................................. | 9 |
| Presbyterian ............................. | 9 |
| Episcopalian ............................. | 8 |
| Seventh-Day Adventist ..................... | 4 |
| Unitarian ............................... | 3 |
| True Mission ............................. | 3 |
| Pentecostal .............................. | 2 |

TABLE IX—PARENTAL STATUS IN HOMES OF 493 BOY AND 16
GIRL TRAMPS

| Parents | Boys | Girls |
|---|---|---|
| TOTAL | 493 | 16 |
| Both parents living | 176 | 4 |
| Both parents dead | 56 | 2 |
| Father dead | 167 | 5 |
| Mother dead | 88 | 3 |
| Divorces | 89 | 3 |
| Separation | 28 | 0 |
| Multiple divorce | 54 | 0 |
| More than 4 divorces | 16 | 0 |
| Stepfather | 62 | 2 |
| Stepmother | 49 | 1 |
| Illegitimate parentage | 37 | 0 |

TABLE X—SIBLING POSITION OF 362 BOY AND 13 GIRL
TRAMPS

| Position | Boys | Girls |
|---|---|---|
| TOTAL | 362 | 13 |
| Middle child | 130 | 3 |
| Oldest | 92 | |
| Youngest | 46 | 7 |
| Only Child | 94 | 3 |

Table XI—Employment Situation in Families of Boy
and Girl Tramps

| Employment Situation | Boys | Girls |
|---|---|---|
| TOTAL | 468 | 9 |
| Father unemployed | 254 | 6 |
| Older brother or sister unemployed | 134 | 1 |
| Father and one other adult brother or sister living at home unemployed | 61 | 0 |
| More than 3 in family unemployed (including father) | 19 | 2 |

Table XII—Period of Parental Unemployment in Homes
of Boy and Girl Tramps Previous to Youth's
Migration

| Period of Parental Unemployment | Boys | Girls |
|---|---|---|
| TOTAL | 247 | 7 |
| Less than 6 months | 2 | 0 |
| 6 months, less than 12 months | 14 | 2 |
| 12 months, less than 18 months | 84 | 1 |
| 18 months, less than 24 months | 61 | 3 |
| 24 months, less than 30 months | 41 | 0 |
| 30 months, less than 36 months | 28 | 0 |
| 36 months and over | 17 | 1 |

TABLE XIII—REASONS FOR LEAVING HOME GIVEN BY BOY AND GIRL TRAMPS

| Reasons for Leaving Home | Boys | Girls |
|---|---|---|
| TOTAL .......................... | 450 | 16 |
| Hard times ....................... | 384 | 3 |
| Trouble with girl .................. | 26 | 0 |
| Liked to travel .................... | 23 | 5 |
| Hated high school ................. | 19 | 4 |
| Going to get married anyway ........ | 3 | 4 |
| Miscellaneous ...................... | 17 | |

TABLE XIV—PERIOD OF MIGRATION OF BOY AND GIRL TRAMPS

| Period of Migration | Boys | Girls |
|---|---|---|
| TOTAL .......................... | 420 | 11 |
| Less than 6 months ................ | 49 | 3 |
| 6 months, less than 12 months ...... | 68 | 0 |
| 12 months, less than 18 months ...... | 119 | 4 |
| 18 months, less than 24 months ...... | 146 | 2 |
| 24 months and over ................ | 38 | 2 |

TABLE XV—ECONOMIC CONDITIONS IN HOMES OF BOY AND GIRL TRAMPS

| Condition | Boys | Girls |
|---|---|---|
| TOTAL .......................... | 496 | 15 |
| Unemployment ................... (parental or sibling) | 388 | 7 |
| On relief ......................... | 69 | 3 |
| Just enough to live on ............. | 32 | 1 |
| Plenty of money .................. | 7 | 4 |

TABLE XVI—EMOTIONAL SITUATION IN HOMES OF A CERTAIN NUMBER OF BOY AND GIRL TRAMPS

| Situation | Boys | Girls |
|---|---|---|
| TOTAL .......................... | 503 | 11 |
| Frequent whippings ............... | 124 | 3 |
| Still liked father .................... | 72 | 0 |
| Still liked mother .................. | 89 | 1 |
| Hated father ....................... | 17 | 1 |
| Hated mother ..................... | 29 | 0 |
| Hated stepfather ................... | 43 | 0 |
| Hated stepmother .................. | 47 | 1 |
| Frequent quarrels with brother ....... | 36 | 1 |
| Frequent quarrels with sister ........ | 29 | 1 |
| Previous wanderings ............... | 17 | 3 |

TABLE XVII—EDUCATION OF BOY AND GIRL TRAMPS

| Highest Grade Reached in School | Boys | Girls |
|---|---|---|
| TOTAL | 504 | 16 |
| Less than 4th grade | 46 | 0 |
| 4th gr., less than 6th grade | 74 | 1 |
| 6th gr., less than 8th grade | 111 | 2 |
| Graduate 8th grade | 143 | 10 |
| Less than 2 years high school | 48 | 2 |
| 2 years, less than 4 years | 31 | |
| Graduate high school | 26 | 1 |
| Less than 2 years college | 17 | |
| 2 years, less than 4 years | 6 | |
| College graduate | 2 | |

TABLE XVIII—NUMBER OF BOY AND GIRL TRAMPS PREVIOUSLY PARTICIPATING IN SCOUT, SUNDAY SCHOOL, OR CLUB WORK

| Activity | Boys | Girls |
|---|---|---|
| TOTAL | 397 | 16 |
| No participation | 265 | 8 |
| Sunday School | 81 | 7 |
| Scout work | 32 | 1 |
| Other clubs | 19 | 0 |

TABLE XIX—OBVIOUS PHYSICAL DEFECTS, CONDITIONS OF
SHOES AND CLOTHES OF A CERTAIN NUMBER OF BOY
AND GIRL TRAMPS

| Condition | Boys | Girls |
|---|---|---|
| Physical Defects .................. | 21 | 2 |
|   A. Hunchback ................... | 5 | 1 |
|   B. One leg ...................... | 2 | 0 |
|   C. Very lame .................. | 4 | 0 |
|   D. Blind in one eye .............. | 6 | 0 |
|   E. Crippled hand or arm .......... | 2 | 0 |
|   F. Disfigured face ............... | 1 | 1 |
| Condition of Clothes: | | |
|   1. Wearable .................... | 121 | 8 |
|   2. Needing repair ............... | 168 | 3 |
|   3. Needing replacement ........... | 201 | 3 |
| Condition of Shoes: | | |
|   1. Serviceable ................. | 72 | 4 |
|   2. Needing repair .............. | 214 | 6 |
|   3. Needing replacement .......... | 298 | 5 |

# GLOSSARY

*accept the Lord*—publicly declare one's belief in God

*accommodation*—a freight train stopping at all stations

*alwaies*—always

*bangs me*—strikes me

*batter privates*—knock on doors of private homes

*big trouble*—the depression

*bindle*—bundle

*black bottle*—a bottle commonly believed to contain a poison which is given to charity patients in a crowded hospital

*blackjack*—a leather-covered weapon filled with lead shot and used as a club

*blind*—the front and unused door of a baggage car: it is nearest the engine and locked

*bonanza wages*—high wages

*brakie*—a brakeman

*brass*—self-confidence

*breaking seals*—breaking the seals on loaded freight cars

*broad*—a woman

*buckles*—heaves and sways

*bull*—lies; policeman

*bullet-like*—very fast

*bull pen*—the place where prisoners are exercised or kept while awaiting trial

*bum*—a homeless man who does not voluntarily work

*bump*—strike; kill; murder

*bunk*—lies; a place to sleep

*bunk on your ears*—sleep on the floor without covering

*burst the mitt*—fracture a hand

*buys no groceries*—makes no money

*canned*—discharged

*cannonading*—going fast

*card*—entertaining person; a meal card

*carry the banner*—walk the streets

*cauliflower*—ears misshapen and bruised

*cell-block*—part of jail

*chain gang* — prisoners wearing shackles on their ankles; any brutal jail

*chair cars*—the transient's iron method of referring to box cars

*chiseling*—cheating

*Christers*—Christians

*clump*—walk heavily

*coaster wagons*—children's play wagons

*coming out of the liquor*—overcoming the effects of intoxication

*cops ain't glimming*—officers are not watching

*couple of*—more than two

*crack*—strike

*crazy quilt*—an illogical array

*creaking the springs*—making too much noise; keeping others awake

*Cripes' sake*—Christ's sake
*cut another's throat* — betray another

*Dago red*—a homemade Italian wine
*day olds*—stale bakery goods
*dehorn alcohol*—denatured alcohol used in automobile radiators
*dodge*—move rapidly; avoid
*dope*—a foolish person
*down the cinders*—along the road bed of a railroad track
*drag*—street
*duck*—avoid
*dumb cluck*—stupid girl
*dummy*—stupid person; the male sex organ
*dump*—house; refuse pile

*empties*—empty box cars

*fairy*—sexual pervert
*fishing*—stealing with a stick and hook
*flip*—jump on
*flop*—a place to sleep
*flop house*—cheap hotel or relief station where the homeless sleep poorly and the bedbugs live well
*freight*—freight train
*frill*—a girl
*front*—respectable appearance
*fruiter*—a sex pervert

*gaffer*—a roustabout worker, usually not much good, and sometimes used derogatorily
*gandy dancer*—an ironworker or steeplejack

*get a girl in trouble*—make a girl pregnant
*get along swell*—succeed
*get burned*—contract a venereal disease
*gives the signal*—the sign to proceed
*glims*—eyes; daylight
*glom*—seize and eat
*glossy-like*—covered over with a mist
*going over the side*—falling from the top of a box car
*gondola*—an open steel coal car
*good front*—well-dressed

*harness bull*—officer in uniform
*heavy-foot*—detective wearing plain clothes but identifiable by his heavy shoes and large feet
*heist*—steal; lift
*hell break loose*—revolution will start
*highball*—signal the brakeman gives to conductor that the train may start
*high-tail*—walk or run
*hit*—strike; beg; ask; panhandle
*hobo*—an itinerant laborer
*hole-up*—remain for the winter, as comfortable as possible
*Home Guard*—a member of the militia who stayed at home during World War, hence any man who remains in one place
*hustle buggy ride*—a ride in a squad car

*jungle*—hobo camp
*just luck*—successful stealing
*kipp*—seize

*ki-yi-ing*—making a noise like a dog

*lambs*—sex perverts: usually young boys used for pleasure by older men
*lammed*—left; struck; stole
*legging*—walking
*line*—conversational ability; a railroad
*look-out*—a place from which one may see the train, or any sentinel post; plural: sentinels

*made his limit*—earned as much as he deemed advisable
*make*—succeed; copulate; acquire
*manifest*—a freight train that does not stop at all towns
*misery*—coffee that has an unpleasant taste
*mulligan*—a stew cooked by tramps in a jungle: generally made out of anything from old shoes to railroad ties, but often palatable and appetizing
*mush talk*—persuasiveness

*nuts*—testicles; crazy

*oke*—from O. K.
*on the fritz*—without attachment; stealing
*on the loose*—wandering
*on the rods*—riding freight trains
*on the street*—soliciting, usually referring to prostitutes
*oyster*—something furnishing one with support

*pearl diving*—washing dishes
*pick lunch*—picnic lunch
*poke*—strike; pocketbook
*power*—engine
*prowl*—steal by stealth
*pull a job*—steal
*put on the low needle*—talk softly

*rat hole*—basement relief station
*red ball*—a freight train having the right of way over a local (*see* manifest)
*red lights*—the segregated district of a city. Here, the red signal lights of a town warning the engineer to slow down. Sometimes used to describe the method by which boy tramps get rid of an unwelcome occupant of a box car: they ask him to look out the door for red lights, and as he does so they kick him
*reefer*—refrigerator car
*rescue*—redemption from sin
*ride passenger*—ride on a passenger train
*ride under cover*—ride inside a box car
*ropes*—method: know the ropes

*Sally's*—at the Salvation Army
*scoffing*—something to eat
*scouts*—reconnoiterers
*shack*—special railroad officer; sometimes a brakeman
*shanty town*—a town composed of shacks built by dispossessed families
*shell out*—give

*silk train*—a train loaded with silk from the Orient

*skating on uppers*—walking on shoes from which heels and soles are worn

*slave market*—location of employment agencies, or the offices themselves

*slug*—money or dollars; strike

*snipe*—pick up from the gutter

*socko*—suddenly

*spiffs*—extra money

*spill the right stuff*—tell a successful story

*stand*—a place to stand and panhandle

*stand the gaff*—endure

*stand up for Jesus*—a public declaration of faith

*stem*—street

*stem is tough*—begging is difficult

*straight sob*—a sad story

*swill*—food fed to transients and hogs

*teakettle*—locomotive engineer

*tender*—coal car immediately behind the engine

*that sin*—perversion

*the silence*—punishment of a child tramp by his companions

*they*—social workers

*throws a fit*—feigns an epileptic attack

*ticket*—a meal ticket; a permit to ride

*tooling ringers*—ringing doorbells

*tramp*—a man who travels but does not work

*tuck*—hide

*vagabundry*—vagabondage

*Wabash Cannonball*—a mythical hobo train

## AMERICANA LIBRARY

*Woman Suffrage and Politics:*
*The Inner Story of the Suffrage Movement*
By Carrie Chapman Catt and Nettie H. Shuler
With a new introduction by T. A. Larson

*The Conquest of Arid America*
By William E. Smythe
With a new introduction by Lawrence B. Lee

*The Territories and the United States, 1861-1890:*
*Studies in Colonial Administration*
By Earl S. Pomeroy
With a new introduction by the author

*Why War*
By Frederic C. Howe
With a new introduction by W. B. Fowler

*Sons of the Wild Jackass*
By Ray Tucker and Frederick R. Barkley
With a new introduction by Robert S. Maxwell

*My Story*
By Tom L. Johnson
With a new introduction by Melvin G. Holli

*The Beast*
By Ben B. Lindsey and Harvey J. O'Higgins
With a new introduction by Charles E. Larsen

*The Liberal Republican Movement*
By Earle D. Ross
With a new introduction by John G. Sproat

*Breaking New Ground*
By Gifford Pinchot
With a new introduction by James Penick, Jr.

*Spending to Save: The Complete Story of Relief*
By Harry L. Hopkins
With a new introduction by Roger Daniels